Low Life

Low Life

THE
SPECTATOR
COLUMNS

Jeremy Clarke

QUARTET

A
CHARLES GLASS
BOOK

First published in 2015 by Charles Glass Books
An imprint of Quartet Books Limited
A member of the Namara Group
27 Goodge Street, London W1T 2LD
A catalogue record for this book
is available from the British Library
ISBN 978 0 7043 7391 4
Typeset by Josh Bryson
Printed and bound in Great Britain by
T J International Ltd, Padstow, Cornwall

CONTENTS

FOREWORD
Jeremy Clarke by Taki

When Jeffrey Bernard died in 1997, the then editor of the *Spectator*, Frank Johnson, declared that there would be no more Low Life. Although the exuberance to honour Bernard was uncharacteristic of Frank Johnson, he meant well. Bernard was a hell of a writer, but his forte was his pathetic life. All day in the pub scrounging drinks, getting into scraps with other drunks, finally falling asleep behind the bar and waking up the morning after having no idea where he was. He and I had written High Life–Low Life for twenty years by the time he expired. I was certain that my term was also coming to an end. High Life needs a Low Life like cops need criminals, in order to justify their existence.

Then came the good news. Boris Johnson discovered someone by the name of Jeremy Clarke, a man of few means who had written for the *Daily Telegraph* an article about karate, one I thoroughly checked in order to find something wrong with it. The writer was a green belt and I am a seven dan, so I was anxious to show my superiority. The trouble was that the green belt got everything right, and also included long, funny passages of how bad he was and how ridiculous it was for him to be trying to play tough guy instead of a comprehending lover. Yes, Jeremy's writings often involve the fairer sex and why not? In a world that has turned topsy-turvy with transgenders and transvestites hogging the headlines, good old-fashioned skirt-chasers like Jeremy are the proverbial breath of fresh air.

Soon afterwards, Jeremy Clarke became Low Life, leaving High Life in the dust with his columns that range from the sublime to the subversive to the superb. Out of the blue he once filed a column from Egypt writing it phonetically, i.e., in the manner people of the Middle East speak English. I remember reading it and remaining dumbfounded. I had been exiled by my father to the Middle East to work in one of his factories, and I know exactly how the people talk. Jeremy had done something that neither Lawrence Durrell nor Cavafy ever managed. Evoking the way foreign people who speak perfect English sound is something I could not achieve in a hundred years of trying. Nor far better writers than yours truly.

Most writers use too many adverbs. Not Jeremy. He keeps it simple. He eschews clichés and drops hints about peoples' inner and outer worlds with nuance and fidelity. He is never frothy, prosy, pedantic or cute. The last even when he tries, as he does time and again when writing about his son and grandson. He sounds like a very, very loving father and granddad. But back to Jeff Bernard for a second. Jeff's friends were a ghastly bunch, drunk and unpleasant. I never met one that I liked. Jeremy's sound wonderful, and the ones I met or talked to over the telephone are all educated and very real people. The only things they lack are billions, which in today's world is a badge of honour.

My real friendship with him began just before the *Spectator* summer party some time ago. I saw him drinking in a pub and told him that 50 yards down the road the drinks were free. But he was drinking to get Dutch courage to greet his fans at the party. Behind the devil-may-care attitude lurks a shy, sensitive soul. But not too shy to write a column that without exaggeration made me scream with laughter. He and a girlfriend are chopping up coke in a low life Spanish dive's communal bathroom. Five or so bursting Spaniards are knocking on the door and trying after awhile to break it down in order to relieve themselves. Still, the girl is methodically chopping up the happy dust while Jeremy's weight against the falling door is the only thing that remains between five furious Spaniards and the coke-cutting lady. Inch by inch the Spaniards advance while Jeremy keeps asking, always very politely, if his lady friend could possibly hurry it up. For me, at least, it was the funniest scene since the Marx brothers shoved 25 unwitting crewmembers into a closet while ordering room service on board an ocean liner in *Monkey Business*.

Then there is his description of a lady friend over Christmas: 'She was wrapped up against the cold, except for her bosoms, which were recklessly exposed and showcased by a black, lacy push'em and point'em out bra.' Then he writes about a friend who had been on a bender to help him get over his grief for his recently deceased brother: 'They had stolen a car and gone on a drug-fueled road trip across three counties wearing pinstriped uniforms and hats stolen from an unattended pizza-delivery company van…' But it's not only drugs, booze and fun with Jeremy. He also writes about F. Scott Fitzgerald's *Tender is the Night*, my bible, like the sensitive and romantic man that he is. His description of the hideous concrete sprawl modern capitalism has wreaked on the once beautiful Riviera coastline is heart-rending.

The last time I saw him was at another *Spectator* party. We then went on to the chicest nightclub of London with my chic friends. He was a nonpareil hit. They had all read him and wanted to know about his cancer. He dismissed it and drank copious amounts of fine French wine. My friends were enchanted by his lack of pretension and love of life. I would go on because I truly love Jeremy, but I can hear him banging on the table and offering me a bottle of absinthe which he once snuck into the Speccie office leaving our sainted editor, Fraser Nelson, speechless. Fraser subsequently wrote an article revealing our combined age and listing the amount of alcohol the two of us consumed in an evening with him.

It's up to you now, readers. A talent such as Jeremy Clarke's is worth introducing, even if it makes me wince at the comparison to my prose.

Taki Theodoracopulos, 2015

GOOD INTENT
20 August 2005

A framed Biblical text hanging on the wall of our home during my growing up years said: 'Flee the evil desires of youth, and pursue righteousness, faith, love and peace, along with those who call on the Lord out of a pure heart' (2 Timothy 2, verse 22). As it sometimes does at incongruous moments, this verse streamed across my mind like an advertising banner towed by a light aircraft. I finished showering, dressed, shouldered my rucksack and quitted the gym. At the café, I asked for cod and chips and a mug of tea, then sat at a table on the warm pavement outside. It was Friday evening. Physically and mentally I felt lean and clean. After a sober fortnight I was the captain of my soul, albeit an unusually diffident one. (Captain's orders: no more smoking, boozing or drugs for the foreseeable future.) The weather forecast for the weekend was unbroken sunshine. I was in credit at the bank. A smiling waitress placed crisply battered cod and chips and a mug of steaming tea before me on the blue-and white check tablecloth. For a rare moment I suspected myself of being what they call happy. I gave thanks and ploughed in.

On the way back to the carpark after I'd eaten, I had to pass the Good Intent, which in fine weather also has tables and chairs set outside on the pavement. This outdoor seating area, an innovation by the new landlord, catches the evening sunshine and has recently become a favourite meeting place for the combination of thugs, slappers, mystics, space cadets, drug dealers and long-term unemployed that passes for the town's jeunesse dorée.

Last week a firm of builders down from London was in town. They were a sociable, free-spending, hard-drinking, coke-snorting gang of blokes and immensely popular, I'd heard it reported, especially with the ladies. One was especially handsome, apparently, and well endowed with it. As I passed by, I looked over and saw that these builders were holding court outside the Good Intent. They were surrounded by the bare midriffs and pierced navels of our local players, and the drink was flowing. I could tell which builder it was they all fancied. He was the short blond one with the big smile for everyone. Sharon, I noted, was in his face, and sitting up and begging like a retriever pleading for a biscuitOnce you've been doing it for a while, it's not easy to stop being a low life. There's nothing people enjoy more than watching someone going to hell on a poker, and they rather resent it if that person suddenly decides he wants to get off. No one objects in principle to an idle, self-centred, addicted life, as long as it ends prematurely in lonely and squalid circumstances and everyone can read about it in the papers. Renege on the deal, like a footballer in mid contract, and people feel cheated.

My fellow low lifes gathered outside the Good Intent somehow spotted my apostasy from right across the road. Maybe it was the medicated shampoo and flyaway hair that gave me away. Perhaps it was the new trainers. Trev came ambling over, put the headlock on me, and literally dragged me back across the road to the pub, where a pint of Stella was thrust into my hand and a lighted fag was put into my mouth. Where had I been lately, they wanted to know. They'd missed me.

Then I was introduced to the builders as if I was some kind of local boozing champion. One of the builders immediately led me inside to the toilet and chopped me up a line of cocaine on one of the cisterns. What time did I call this, he said. I had a lot of catching up to do, he said. I could have refused, I suppose. I could have argued that I was more of a speed freak than a coke tart. But the captain of my soul had now locked himself in his cabin and was refusing to come out.

After we'd snorted the lines of coke, and religiously hoovered up the crumbs, he lifted the lavatory lid and unzipped his fly. And as he did so he did a surprisingly good imitation of a U-boat klaxon signalling an emergency.

Of course I got into the swing of it quite quickly after that. I bought more rounds of drinks than even the builders and they all said what a fine fellow I was. The handsome one became quite emotional about it. But lying awake in the footwell of my car at five o'clock next morning, cold, ill and repentant, how I wished I'd heeded the warning in the shower and spent the evening pursuing righteousness, faith, love and peace instead of that.

WELCOME TO CAIRO
6 May 2008

We first encountered Ahmed, our dragoman in Cairo, when he stepped forward to greet us at pass-port control. He was dressed soberly in dark suit, black tie, black shoes. Shaved head. Designer glasses. His manner was brisk and unsmiling. But now and again an engagingly complicit smile lighted his hawkish face to remind us that he understood as well as we that all is vanity.

He expedited the entry formalities then led us outside to a waiting people carrier and slid back the door for us. Ahmed sat up in front, beside the driver. The driver spoke no English and gave his full attention to the road ahead. Ahmed, on the other hand, was very comfortable with the language and liked to talk. The hotel was on the far side of the city.

'Welcome to Cairo. What do you think of Cairo traffic? It is the worst in the world. If you will notice, there are no rules. Can you tell me which is the fast lane? You cannot. Every lane is the fast lane. Traffic lights? What are these? They are just for decoration — like Christmas. I have friends who have been to Mexico, to Athens, to Rome. They say that Cairo traffic is worse. What are you doing? That seat belt is maybe not working. Sorry. But don't worry! Amr is a very good driver. He is a Christian. A Copt. Look! The Copt is smiling. I am Muslim, he is Christian. You are surprised? Egypt is a very old country. We respect one another. We respect other religions. We are

4

not Iraq. 'Please smoke if you want to. Please. Go ahead. In Egypt the people make the rules, not the government. We don't respect the government. The Egyptian government is 100 per cent corrupt. In other countries the government is 10 per cent corrupt or maybe 20 or 50 per cent. Here in Egypt it is 100 per cent corrupt. I am telling you.

'Mubarak is a piece of shit. He is nothing. Noth-thing. You know what we call Mubarak? Rameses the Third. You have heard of the Pharoah Rameses the Third? Rameses the Third ruled Egypt for 69 years. Mubarak wants to beat him. We don't care about the government. Excuse my language. We don't give a shit about them. Egypt is a police state, but the government is scared of the people. So we ignore them and make our own rules. You see how even traffic as crazy as this stops for this one old woman? We respect each other. But we don't respect the government. Please. Go ahead and smoke if you want to.

'Now we are passing through a graveyard. Many tombs. Many dead people. Look. On both sides, a huge graveyard. The biggest graveyard in Cairo. This road was very controversial when it was new. So many children live in this graveyard there are now two schools. You want some fresh pollution? Let me wind down the window a little and let in some fresh pollution. Why should we stop smoking in Cairo when we breathe in smoke all the time. We need cigarettes to flavour the smoke a little.

'If you look on the right, this is the mosque of Mohammed Ali. Not the boxer. The ruler. Very famous mosque. I think that the traffic today is worse even than usual. By the way that man drives, he is Russian. So many people are killed driving off this bridge at night, the police close it after mid-night. We need a better one. But let me tell you what will happen. In Saudi Arabia if they want to build a bridge, in six months they have a shiny new bridge. In Syria when they want a new bridge, it is completed after two years, but the quality of the bricks has been compromised because of some government corruption. In Egypt all the money is stolen and the bridge is not even started.

'But we don't care about the government. We are an ancient people. A tolerant people. A peaceful people. Europeans ask me if Cairo is safe. It makes me laugh. Cairo is safe. You can walk around and even if you are a sexy woman no one will touch you. If you want help, everybody will rush to help you. My friend went to Paris and was robbed on the street by a woman with a knife. In Paree! This woman who robbed her had metal objects in her face: here, here and here. Like a circus. This would never happen in Cairo. Is it safe? Don't make me laugh. Now we are crossing the Nile.'

I looked down at the sacred Nile, about a mile wide at this point, confident already that I was going to like Egypt very much indeed.

AN ABSOLUTE SHOCKER
10 March 2010

When the relationship ended a week before the Christmas before last, she'd already bought my Christmas presents. Instead of posting or burning them, she stored them under the desk in her of-fice, resting her exquisite feet on them during working hours, until three weeks ago, when we final-ly met again over a tapas in a Spanish restaurant off the Edgware Road, and she managed to hand over, after some 14 months, the carrier bag containing her parting gifts.

One was a hardback copy of Everyday Drinking by Kingsley Amis. I read it straight off when I got home and loved it. It's a boozer's manual, informative and funny. The chapter on hangovers I found particularly fascinating. In it, he describes the various aspects of the hangover and suggests a few strategies for coping with them. As well as describing the physical hangover, which of course he did so brilliantly and memorably in Lucky Jim, interestingly he then goes on to describe and analyse what he calls the 'metaphysical' hangover.

The metaphysical hangover, he says, is the spiritual desolation which invariably accompanies the well-known physical collapse. Of the two aspects, he thinks the metaphysical hangover is the uglier customer. Whereas the headache and nausea begin to lessen around mid-afternoon, the terrible depression, anxiety, sadness, sense of failure and fear of the future of the metaphysical hangover seem permanent. His advice is always to bear in mind that this spiritual malaise is merely a hangover and nothing worse, and that it too will eventually go.

He does, however, recommend having 'a good cry' at some stage. He also suggests reading the final scene of Paradise Lost, Book VII, and then a battle poem or two, such as Chesterton's 'Lepanto'. 'Try not to mind,' he says, 'the way Chesterton makes some play with the fact that this was a victory of Christians over Moslems.'

I have always found my moral collapse during a hangover to be far more horrifying than the nausea and have always wondered whether it was because I lacked gravitas. I was therefore glad to see such an unimpeachable source as Kingsley Amis describing the symptoms so accurately, dignifying the condition with a respectable name, and candidly admitting to a moral collapse as bad, if not worse, than mine.

And what I am getting to, finally, is that I am stricken with one humdinger of Mr Amis's metaphysical hangovers right now, this morning, as I write.

Last night was Trevor's 50th birthday party. Before last night I hadn't touched a drop since the port and Jack Daniels I had with Rod Liddle on New Year's Day, and I knew I was going to pay a heavy price. As I got ready to go to the party, I looked in the bathroom mirror and apologised to myself in advance for trashing myself after so many weeks of diligent abstinence.

It was a proper party, as expected. The intoxicants available were plentiful and various. When I left Trev's house at dawn it was still going strong. Everything that one associates with and could possibly hope for at an all-night party happened, with the possible exception of intervention by riot police. Sharon was there. No one had seen her for ages. The excitement generated by her arrival reminded me of a diva coming out of retirement for a special gala performance. She'd been on the wagon, too, for several months and, as we all expected, she didn't just fall off, she double-somersaulted off with half-twist and pike. Fortunately for everybody present, her usual transition from amorousness to mindless aggression to unconsciousness was mercifully rapid. Unusually for me, I pulled, I think. By the time she comes out of school this afternoon Tory will probably have forgotten about the tearful promises we made to each other last night in the heat of the moment, but if she hasn't, and she still wants her sugar daddy to buy her an iPhone, I have a new girlfriend.

As metaphysical hangovers go, this one's a shocker. I've taken Kingsley Amis's advice and had a good cry. And I've read 'Lepanto', taking into account the surprising fact that, as he points out, the naval victory over the Turks in 1571 was achieved without the help of a single Anglo-Saxon or Protestant. Yes, it's a stirring poem, but what's a stirring poem to me when I'm dying of shame and a brain lesion and I've come at last to see life as it really is?

ROTTEN LUCK
19 March 2011

Beside the roundabout a woman was standing with her thumb out. Late thirties. Black knee-length boots. Old jeans. No coat. The thumb was resigned, indifferent.

I swung in sharply, positioning the door handle precisely level with the thumb. She pulled the door open and sat in. A red, careworn face. I stated my destination. She said she would ride with me as far as Graves Cross. I clicked the lever into drive and we set off up the hill.

Silence. She stared resignedly ahead. If hitch-hikers prefer not to speak, it's fine. I'm not one of those who feel they are owed an explanation or a potted biography. I usually have the music turned up in any case. But this woman's indifferent, fatalistic air impressed me. I strongly sensed a woman hemmed in by bullshit and poverty; a woman expecting nothing from life but more of the same; a woman without a single life-enhancing delusion. I respectfully asked her where she had been today.

She had been to the Job Centre, she said, keeping her eyes on the road. She'd been 'on the sick' for five years, but now that she was well, she was obliged to present herself there for an interview. The Job Centre woman had solemnly promised that any job they found for her would pay a minimum of eight pounds a week more than her combined housing and unemployment benefit. It had cost her more than that, she observed drily, to travel there to be told it.

I asked her why she had been 'on the sick'. Cancer, she said. Ovaries. They'd ripped it all away, she said: womb, ovaries, the lot. Had she children? I said. One, she said. A boy. Now 22 years of age. She was glad she'd borne a child while she could. He's in there, actually, she said, cocking a thumb. We were passing the turn-off for the prison. He was doing life, she said.

What for? I said. Street robbery, she said. Rather a hefty sentence for street robbery, surely? I said. It's an effing joke, she said. It was true that her son had a backlog of other convictions and charges, none of them particularly serious. But he hadn't committed no street robbery. He was just doing his job. Which was? Collecting protection money, she said. His client had refused to pay up and her son had beaten him. The client went to the police claiming he'd been the victim of a street robbery. He chose his false accusation with care. Judges come down heavily on street robbery.

Goodness me, it all sounds most unjust, I said, with the uncomfortable feeling that every supplementary question of mine was ushering us inexorably into a lower circle of hell. So what was the nature of her son's client's business? Drugs, she said. Smack. A dealer. In return for his weekly payment her son had protected him from 'hassle'. I expect this drug dealer isn't looking forward to your son's release very much, I said. He's disappeared, she said, her eyes still on the road.

Blooming drugs, I said, carefully overtaking a toiling cyclist. They're an absolute curse. She agreed with me up to a point. She had to have her smoke, she said. If she didn't have her daily spliff, people had better look out.

11

What happens if you don't have it? I said. Basically, she loses her temper, she said. For example? For example there was that time when someone gave her 'grief' in the street about her son. She'd followed him into the fish and chip shop and bitten his ear off. She hadn't meant to bite it off. She'd only meant to scream into it. But she hadn't had a smoke that day, and in her blind temper she hadn't realised she was chewing on the ear at the same time.

Dear me, I said. What rotten luck. Surely there were consequences? Oh, yes, she said. When he'd tried to hit her, she'd bitten his finger off, too. Three and a half years she'd got for that. She rattled off the names of four of Her Majesty's prisons as though they were illustrious household names. I hadn't heard of three of them.

I looked at her. She was still looking ahead. The face was placid. It was perhaps an often told tale. We'd only scratched the surface. The hinterland was vast. That was the impression.

We arrived at the crossroads where she said she was getting out, and I pulled over. Well, it's been nice talking to you, I said. She looked at me, considered me as though for the first time, then dismissed me with a half-suppressed snort of derision. But when she got out there was a degree of gratitude, I felt, in the way she was careful not to slam the door.

NATIONAL CLEAVAGE DAY

30 June 2011

We've ridden African elephants and done the evening game drive. In between I've had the full-body Swedish massage from a Zulu woman who used the point of her elbow and the side of her knee and was panting slightly throughout. Now we are six of us around a dinner table in a replica Zulu meeting hut. The waiters are Pedi.

With each course a different wine is poured. My neighbour vulgarly asks the cost of the first, a silky red, and is told that it isn't on the wine list. However, a bottle from the same vineyard, of an inferior vintage, can be had for the equivalent of £400. I'm studiously trying to keep up with these various wines and remember which is which. But I'm reserving my greater seriousness for the succession of Tequila Sunrises being placed in front of me in glasses about a foot tall.

There was a Tequila Sunrise among an imaginative selection of drinks on the welcome-back-to-camp tray after the afternoon game drive. I was attracted by the trippy colours and the ridiculous size of the glass. Later, when we assembled on the decking beside the crocodile pool for pre-dinner drinks, I told the Pedi waiter I'd like another one of those colourful jobs.

These Pedi waiters are stalwart chaps. When I said I was a lifelong admirer of their formidable illegitimate warrior-king Sekhukhune, they couldn't have been more pleased. Since then they've treated me like a brother.

I've carried my unfinished Tequila Sunrise to the dinner table and moments after I've drained it, one of them is bending at my shoulder, whispering respectfully in my ear about having another one. There isn't a trace of irony or derision in his manner. My unhesitating assent gladdens him, and he keeps them coming all evening.

Near the end, for afters, the sommelier announces Napoleon Bonaparte's favourite wine, a potent little number from the historic wine-growing district of Constantia. I'm not overly keen on wine, no matter how expensive, but I'm with Napoleon on this one. It's yellow, sweet and numbs the nut nicely. The Pedi waiter totes the bottle around the table, carefully tipping it into our smallest wine glass. I sling mine back in one as soon as he stops pouring. Proud of me, he immediately pours me another. The general manager is with Napoleon on this one, too. A discreet, fanatical nod from him and the waiters are wrestling the cork out of a second, then a third bottle. By the time coffee is being mooted, I might not be thinking about invading Botswana, but I'm certainly ready to hit the nearest town, if there is one.

The game reserve covers 30,000 hectares and shares fences with other game reserves. But during last night's game drive I'd noticed a sprinkling of lights on the horizon, enough lights perhaps to warrant a bar. I mention it now to the assembly, and the general manager rallies immediately to the standard. Yes, there is a town, he says. It is about half an hour away by safari truck. A mere spit. And in the town there is indeed a bar, which should be quite lively, it being both a Saturday night and National Cleavage Day. He'd be more than happy to drive us there, he says. We should go.

The town is a small Afrikaner dorp called Vaalwater, he adds. The literal translation of Vaalwater is 'murky water'. The bar will probably be packed with Afrikaner farm boys and girls getting properly drunk and doing that one-armed waltz that they do. So be warned, he says, the ambience might be more agricultural than some of us are used to.

As far as I am concerned, I cannot think of anything in this world that I would rather do at this moment than drive for half an hour across the veld, under midnight stars, to a bar choc-full of Afrikaner farm boys and girls, all smashed out of their minds on a Saturday night and waltzing as their forefathers used to do. I rise to my feet. Take us to Murky Water's most self-consciously Boer bar on this your National Cleavage Day, I say to the general manager, and our lives will be complete.

The eventual line-up for the trip to town is the general manager in the driving seat, me, and one of the Pedi waiters, sleepy now, who slips down from the truck on the outskirts and vanishes into the darkness. Vaalwater's bar is emblazoned with light and inside all is exactly as the general manager had predicted. Not a black, an old or even a partially sober face. I shoulder my way politely through the imprecise dancing and a woman behind the bar ambles over to take my order. The expression is neither welcoming nor hostile. 'Laager, please, darling,' I tell her.

COWBELLS
19 March 2011

Early on Sunday morning the phone rang. Trev. He could hardly speak because his ribs hurt so much, he said. And I should see his face. One eye was closed, he had a deep gash across his forehead and a chunk had been taken out of the top of his nose. But how had it happened? One minute he was walking home alone from the disco, and the next he'd woken up in bed and found himself in this terrible state. Did I know what had happened to him? And where did I disappear to, anyway? One minute I was there, he said, next to him on the dance floor, and the next I was gone.

I'd left early to catch the night sleeper to Paddington, then the Heathrow Express to Terminal 1, I said. I was sorry, I said, but I had absolutely no idea what had happened to him. I last saw him on the dance floor, throwing shapes.

'So where are you now?' he said. I looked out of the train carriage window at the spark-ling blue lake and the mountains beyond. 'Lake Geneva,' I said. 'Oh. Right,' he said. He sounded disappointed. 'Where's that?' 'Switzerland,' I said. 'Oh,' he said.

Three hours later our travelling party was having lunch outside a wooden 18th-century farmer's hut in a sunny meadow overlooking Gstaad. Our hosts were Andrea and Laura Scherz, owners of the Gstaad Palace hotel. The hut's interior was equipped simply and cosily as a kind of romantic hideaway available to their hotel guests.

16

The conversation was lively and gay in the thin air. Mrs Scherz was funny, describing a visit with her young children to a pop concert at the O2 stadium last October, while all manner of meats, hot and cold, were deftly forked on to our plates by an Italian waiter wearing a smock embroidered with meadow flowers; then we helped ourselves to local cheeses, pastries, ice cream and strawberries. I could have drunk the light white wine all day long.

So did they know Taki, I said? (Taki has a home in Gstaad.) The Scherz's handsome faces lit up with sheer delight at the mere mention of the name. Why, yes indeed, of course they knew Taki. He is a very fit, very active man, they said. He is a tennis player and keen hill walker, and presenter each year of the Taki Cup for the fastest ascent of Wasserngrat (the steepest mountain in Gstaad) on snowshoes. But above all Taki is a fun person, they said. And there was a brief pause as the gates of a magnificent treasure house of Taki-inspired anecdotes stood open before them, and they hardly knew where to begin.

Did I know, for example, that Taki was the first in Gstaad to own one of the new Mini Coopers, said Mr Scherz? Taki drove it around Gstaad drawing universal admiration until he drove it one afternoon into a tree in the town centre. (Mr Scherz demonstrated with his hands the girth of this tree.) Taki of course had had a sherbert or two and so smartly absented himself from the scene.

As a great believer myself in doing a runner from these kinds of situations, I murmured strong approval. Mr Scherz's answering smile was not disapproving either.

And where did Taki go? Where else but to the Gstaad Palace, said Mr Scherz. However, word quickly got out that the outlaw had sought refuge in the Palace lounge and a policewoman celebrated locally for her great beauty was dispatched to apprehend him. She marched in, spotted him immediately, and as she was about to feel his collar, Taki made two last requests. One was that he be allowed five minutes alone with her upstairs wearing only her boots. The other that he be permitted to bring his bust of Mussolini with him down to the nick for moral support.

We laughed and laughed in the warm Alpine sunshine. And it was really quite something to see their faces alight with affection and pleasure as they recalled the escapade of a much-loved neighbour. And Taki, I'd like to add my own affectionate wishes to those of Andreas and Laura Scherz for your speedy recovery from last week's infirmity.

After lunch my phone rang again. Trev — his breathing laboured. After he'd rung me earlier, he gasped, he'd noticed that he was wearing a hospital wristband. So that must mean he had been seen by a doctor. If he can walk, said Trev, he planned to return to the casualty department and try to find out what has happened to him.

I was sure I didn't know anything? Quite sure, I said. And what was that noise in the background, he said? Cowbells, I said.

'Oh,' he said.

GREEN FAIRY
30 June 2011

No prizes for guessing who wrote this, or what the drink is:

> 'There was very little left of it [in his hipflask] and one cup of it took the place of the evening papers, of all the old evenings in the cafés, of all the chestnut trees that would be in bloom now in this month, of the great slow horses of the outer boulevards, of bookshops, and kiosks, and of galleries, and of the Parc Montsouris, of the Stade Buffalo, and of the Butte Chaumont, of Foyet's old hotel, and of being able to relax and read in the evening, of all the old things he had enjoyed and forgotten and that came back to him when he tasted that opaque, bitter, tongue numbing, brain warming, stomach warming, idea changing liquid alchemy.'

When Ernest Hemingway (the sentence is from *For Whom the Bell Tolls*) and Hadley crossed the Atlantic in 1921, absinthe had been banned in France for six years. The ban was the result of lobbying from a jealous wine industry and a moral panic based on absinthe's reputation as a hallucinogenic. La Fée Verte (the Green Fairy) has always been legally available in Spain, however, which was where Hemingway later prosecuted his love affair with the stuff.

But was absinthe hallucinogenic? Here's Oscar Wilde on the subject:

Three nights I sat up all night drinking absinthe, and thinking I was clearheaded and sane. The waiter came in and began watering the sawdust. The most wonderful flowers — tulips, lilies and roses — sprang up and made a garden of the café. 'Don't you see them?' I said to him. 'But Monsieur, there is nothing there.'

Last month, France's teetotal President Sarkozy announced the lifting of the ban after nearly a century. It's always splendid when a small measure of personal liberty that has been peremptorily removed is suddenly and unexpectedly handed back. But searching the web for somewhere to place my order, I was surprised to learn that authentic, artisanal, pre-ban recipe French absinthe intended for the export market has been manufactured in France for more than a decade: first by La Fée, a British company, then with French distillers following suit. More surprising still, I learned that these pre-ban French recipe absinthes are and have been easily obtainable because the legendary tipple has never been banned over here either.

Last Bank Holiday weekend I took a bottle of French made pre-ban recipe absinthe round to Sharon's house. The line-up around the kitchen table was as follows: Sharon, Sharon's brother, Sharon's father, Sharon's brother's girlfriend, and me. It was a Sunday evening. Sharon was feeling crapulent. Everyone was yawning. I placed before us a bottle of Grande Absinte, 69% ABV, made with star anise, wormwood, mugwort and lemon balm.

Sharon's brother drank the first glass. He plays rugby. In spite of my entreaties to keep things civilised and responsible, he downed half a tumbler neat. His head tilted slowly back to catch the dregs, then catapulted forward, and he sat with his chin on his chest, paralysed, and we all thought that was the end of him.

But after about half a minute he lifted his head, and with tears standing out in his eyes pronounced it 'not bad'. The rest of us took ours in the more traditional, sedate manner, diluted with water trickled over a sugar lump suspended above the glass on a perforated absinthe spoon.

We had a wonderful, argumentative and occasionally dramatic evening. After about three glasses each, Sharon's dog Django, a Weimaraner, came charging into the kitchen and tried to kill Sharon's brother's dog, a boxer called Watson, and it took all five of us to prise them apart. 'He never liked Boxson,' was the sad verdict of Sharon's dad. It was the last thing he said before he passed out in his chair, toppling over and falling to the floor with a tremendous crash, and we all had to look lively again, grab hold of a limb each and carry him to the nearest sofa.

After about glass number four everyone was standing up and shouting at one another and Sharon was crying, and I can remember noting with surprise a feeling of utter peace, clarity and self-possession, as though my mind wasn't impaired by the alcohol in the slightest, rather that I was at my alert and perceptive best. Next morning, with this feeling of clarity and imperturbability still on me, I stepped on something hard and sharp. It was the upper set of Sharon's dad's false teeth lying abandoned on the living room carpet.

Afterwards I rang George Rowley, managing director of La Fée absinthe. We hadn't seen tulips, I said, nor carthorses on boulevards. I had however attained an unusual mental clarity, and I had found it very agreeable. I was absolutely converted, I said. But how far should I attribute the unusual clarity I experienced to the wormwood?

Mr Rowley said that he thought that in any discussion of absinthe's singular effects, 'wormwood is a red herring'. He thought them more likely due to a combination of factors, including the exceptionally high alcohol content, the dilating effect of anise on the capillaries, the psychoactive effect of all the herbs, not just the wormwood, and perhaps most importantly the anticipation of the drinker as the drink is prepared.

It's true. That slowly passing minute, as the cold water trickles on to the sugar cube, and the sweetness dribbles down through the perforations in the absinthe spoon, turning the clear, emerald spirit to an opaque milky whiteness, as though by sacramental magic, does raise expectations — to a fever pitch, if you are easy prey to the absurdities thrown up by a romantic imagination.

'Idea changing, liquid alchemy,' said old Ernesto, via his fictional hero Robert Jordan. I'm not sure about that. I'll let you know. But a weird clarity of mind that seems the very opposite of drunkenness — that I can vouch for.

OLD BIKER
28 August 2011

In summer the cottage next door is let out to visitors. Each week there's someone new. I see them coming and going and sometimes circumstances dictate that I get to meet them. Last week a man staying in the cottage came to the door to ask about the television signal in the village. It wasn't very good, was it? This visitor spoke with a Welsh accent and limped.

Reception does vary a bit according to the weather, I said, but our signal seemed fairly strong at the moment. Theirs was fine at the beginning of the week, he said, but now the picture was breaking up on all freeview channels. This morning they'd had to abandon the *Jeremy Kyle Show* and watch *Homes Under the Hammer* on BBC1, which they weren't keen on, to be honest, and now even BBC1 was unwatchable. It was very disappointing to come away on holiday and find the telly not working. If his daughter couldn't watch *Holby City* later in the week, look out, he said.

Life is too short, surely, I thought, to be watching Homes Under the Hammer on a beautiful summer's day. But I made sympathetic noises and said I'd pop round and have a look at their telly. With my long experience of poor reception, I said, I should be able to determine at a glance whether atmospherics were indeed to blame.

Fifteen minutes later I was welcomed into their sitting room and he introduced me to his wife, who was placidly knitting, his daughter and his son-in-law. The four of them were seated in a homely semi-circle around what my father used to call the idiots' lantern. I now saw that the man's limp had been caused by his artificial leg, which he had now removed for greater comfort when seated in an easy chair in front of the telly. His good leg was folded easily under his stump. The flesh-coloured plastic leg was propped against the wall.

They'd turned back to ITV, to the Jeremy Kyle Show. The pattern of disintegration was all too familiar. 'It's the signal, definitely,' I said. I checked the connection at the aerial socket. It seemed fine. Then I saw another, unused aerial socket on the other side of the room and I suggested we gave that a try in case the source was stronger. The one-legged man slid off the chair on to the floor and propelled himself across the carpet with a kind of unorthodox swimming stroke. The strength, vigour and rapidity of his movements were surprising and impressive. He got to the socket first and closely examined it from his ground-level perspective.

I couldn't help myself. 'What happened to your leg?' I said. 'I lost it in a motorbike accident years ago,' he said. 'I've been without it longer than I had it.' 'What was the bike?' I said. 'Only a little BSA — a 250,' he said. His face, as he looked up at me from the floor, was a little ashamed.

Once a British biker always a British biker, I thought admiringly. Even after all these years he's still apologising to people for allowing such an inoffensive bike to do him such a substantial amount of damage. He and I talked British bikes for a while. His wife continued to knit placidly. Daughter and son-in-law stared doggedly at the disintegrating picture.

24

I never had a motorbike, British or otherwise, but I once drank in a biker pub in Essex and sometimes rode on the back of a Norton Commando. The pub clientele struck me as well-adjusted, but on the road they must have been a bunch of lunatics because so many were killed or maimed in motorbike accidents in a short time that a television company came down and made a documentary about the pub. I told him that. And I told him that until my late twenties the only friends and acquaintances who died young did so as a result of motorcycle accidents, the details of which were mostly horrific.

I don't suppose the statistics have got any better over the years now that it is a question not of how fast does the bike go, but have you the strength to hang on to the handlebars, I said. What happened to him and his BSA, I said. Was it a bad smash?

His wife looked up from her knitting. 'He fell off at the traffic lights and a lorry ran over him,' she said pleasantly. It was a long time ago yet shame coloured his face again. And looking up at me, as he was, from a prone position on the floor, he looked terribly abject.

IRISH EYEBROWS
7 September 2011

The pub was taken over for a meeting. Every chair was occupied. The speaker's words were being recorded by a sound engineer standing at a portable mixing console. The middle-aged audience was rapt, the atmosphere one of political and moral seriousness. Few were drinking. I mounted the only vacant bar stool and mouthed the word 'Peroni' at the young lad behind the bar as though he and I were involved in a dangerous conspiracy.

The speaker, a woman aged around 50, was speaking articulately and authoritatively about something called the blood/brain barrier. To sustain it, she said, we need to maintain adequate levels of fatty acids, vitamin D and particularly iodine, which most people fail to do. Every woman in the West was iodine-deficient and their brains weren't working propcily, she said.

Recently she'd spent time in Ireland. She'd never in all her life seen so many people showing signs of a compromised blood/brain barrier. The statistics, she said, were that one in three of the Irish population had some kind of brain-related health issue. A telltale symptom of iodine deficiency is a shortening of the eyebrows. In Ireland, she said, the number of people with shortened eyebrows is amazing.

I looked at the audience. There was something like devotion in its engrossed attention. And who could blame them? All we seem to get these days is bad or misinformation, advertising disguised as fact, ideology disguised as truth, propaganda even. It was all so confusing. Who or what lay behind it all? But here at last was an undeceived woman with an intact blood/brain barrier, possibly the only one left in the Western world, telling them what sounded spookily like the truth.

But, for me, that eyebrow business put a big dent in her thesis. I'm a huge fan of the medical model for an explanation of human behaviour. It beats politics, for example, hands down. But the disappearance of eyebrows in Ireland, like a biblical plague, and coming on top of all their other recent problems, seemed scarcely credible. I sipped my beer sceptically.

What is happening in Ireland is starting to happen over here, she said. Without iodine to strengthen and nourish our blood/brain barriers, all sorts of toxins and metals are getting through, resulting in universal brain damage. Fluoride is one, aluminium another. And if that wasn't bad enough, our brains are under sustained assault from the electromagnetic cloud generated by mobile phones, microwave ovens and home computers. The electromagnetic cloud is a negative charge. Our brains thrive on a positive charge; the best, most natural source of which is the earth under our feet.

Of course, the native American Indians knew this. Of course they did. If someone was sick they dug a hole in the ground, filled it with grass and laid them in it, trusting in the healing power of the earth. In her own healing practice, for most types of illness she recommends walking barefoot in the dew in the mornings. (She tells them to walk backwards, because the footfall is more complete.)

After that the speaker seemed to me to cast off all pretence of rationality and even plausibility. Our compromised blood/brain barriers are the result of a conspiracy between the government, the medical profession and the pharmaceutical industry. The earth has a heartbeat, which is increasing in rapidity. In 1911 it was 7.4. Today it is up near 11. The HIV virus is a myth put about to promote the Aids industry.

But we needn't despair. Society is changing. The earth is travelling in a part of the universe saturated with health-giving, consciousness-changing photons. The pharmaceutical companies and 'powers that be' know this. That is why they are currently doing everything in their power to prevent us getting that photon-electron attachment to our cells. But they can't prevent us from going barefoot! They can't asphalt over the entire planet! Here, spontaneous applause broke out. The audience was absolutely lapping it up. They might be brain-damaged but they were still the local intelligentsia and they could still recognise truth when they heard it. But I'd heard enough. I knocked back the dregs of my beer and made for the door.

In the street outside, I ran straight into the man with probably the most compromised blood/brain barrier in Britain today: Trev — en route from one pub to another. It was Sunday evening and his pallor suggested that the traffic of toxins between his blood and his brain had been heavy in both directions all weekend. He got me in a tight clinch. 'Dude,' he whispered in my ear. 'I've got something really nice in my pocket.'

COUNTRY LIFE
1 October 2011

Somewhat frayed around the edges after *The Spectator*'s 'End of Summer Party' I drove up to Norfolk to visit my country cousins. The corpses on the A143 told me I was getting deeper into the countryside. As well as the usual pea-brained pheasants, I saw a bloody badger, a broken fox and a magnificent, unmarked hare that was bigger than either of these. Normally, I would have stopped and taken the fox's brush as a present for my grandson, but there was a car up my arse.

I stayed with my uncle and aunt on their smallholding and was given my usual bed in a spare room that doubles as an egg-packing station. Quite often I wake in the night not knowing where I am. I sit bolt upright in the darkness in an existential panic trying to figure it out. If I've been dreaming, I think I'm in a railway tunnel or a mineshaft or I'm looking out from a cave. The prosaic, less frightening truth, when I realise it, that I am in a bedroom, lying on a bed, comes as a huge relief. But when I wake at my uncle and aunt's place, and look round in a panic, and all I can see are eggs, and the silhouettes of eggs, thousands of them, in trays, stacked around me, it takes a while to realise that here in Norfolk reality can be every bit as bizarre as a dream.

At my uncle and aunt's place you are fully in the country. You eat the best bacon and eggs imaginable, the dogs are kept outside, the well-thumbed books on the shelf are about pig breeding and chicken breeds, the latest edition of Cage and Aviary Bird lies on the arm of the chair, and the talk is mostly of the predations, infections, contaminations and atrocities committed by vermin such as mice, rats, mink, sparrowhawks, crows, foxes, badgers.

Since I was last up there, otters have been added to the list. The only reason that otters have been painstakingly reintroduced into East Anglia, encouraged to breed, and protected by stringent laws, apparently, is to antagonise hardworking, Conservative-voting smallholders with ornamental lakes and ponds. Bold as brass, and conscious, perhaps, of their protected, minority status, these upstart otters are going from one private lake to the next stripping them of valuable fish. Only last week the 'cheeky devils' cleaned out my uncle's neighbour's pond of ornamental carp, all old monsters.

It's the same with the hawks and raptors. The powerful RSPB lobbies for their continued protection and with no predators such as my uncle and his rook rifle to worry about they've proliferated to an absurd extent. And then we read about declining songbird numbers, says my uncle, indignation raising his voice by an octave or two.

As for the explosion in the badger population, well, it's best not to mention it and start my uncle off. But I do anyway. I tell my uncle I've read an official pamphlet in which all the submissions to the previous government's inquiry into the badger/TB issue were collected and summarised. In it, I tell him, some badger protection groups were of the opinion that it was the badgers who were being infected by the cows, rather than vice versa, and the cows were being infected in the first place by farmers and their farm labourers.

My uncle has been quite poorly lately. Sometimes he thinks he's nearing the end and jokes that he is planning no further forward than his next change of shirt. But when I tell him things like that, the world is suddenly so far beyond his understanding, and the people in it so wilfully ignorant, that he is almost glad to be going. As for all that free-range egg business, he took me to see one of his son's free-range chicken sheds, to show me what a lot of nonsense it is. 'Look in there,' he said. I opened a door, looked in, and was confronted with a flock of 5,000 brown hens standing in a shed, all craning their necks and staring at me as though I was mad. The sun was shining, the doors were open, they had five lovely green acres to play in, yet they all preferred to be indoors. 'They feel safer inside,' my uncle explained. 'Outside they feel vulnerable to attack by hawks. Even if a seagull drifts over they all run for cover. Give me a battery-cage egg any day,' he confided. 'You know it's clean and it tastes the same as an egg produced any other way.'

I profoundly disagree. At home we eat eggs laid by chickens scratching around in the earth for insects and there's no comparison. And I think battery cages are an abomination. But not wanting my uncle to lump me in with the sentimentalists, I kept quiet.

REGATTA!
3 October 2011

I took my grandson, Oscar, 20 months old, down to the regatta on the bus, a double-decker, his first experience of one, and we sat upstairs at the front. The bus was far too big for the narrow country lanes and the overhanging branches of trees thrashed against the upstairs windows.

We alighted at a bus stop in the middle of the festivities, beside a funfair in full swing. The tipsy bank holiday crowd, the flags, the bunting, the lines of orange police cones, and the bright yellow fixed-penalty notice stuck on the side window of almost every visible parked car, made for a colourful scene.

We hadn't been there more than a minute when a precise naval officer's voice on the loudspeakers announced the arrival of a Hawker Sea Fury over the town. Presently a plane similar in shape to a Spitfire appeared and performed a series of loop the loops right above our heads. After that the chap on the loudspeaker announced a one-minute silence so we stood quietly and still for that, the rain gently pattering the stretched fabric of our borrowed umbrella. The silence was a mark of respect for the Red Arrows pilot killed earlier in the week. The Red Arrows have performed at the regatta for as long as I can remember. Not this year. The difference between a Red Arrows display and a minute's silence was stark.

After the silence, granddad's bladder told him it needed emptying, so we made our way, via the funfair, to the public convenience next to the river. Oscar tripped and trotted along beside me, his small hand in mine. Perhaps I should say here that the more I get to know Oscar, the more I respect him. When the Chinese sage Lao-tzu said, 'He who possesses virtue may be compared to an infant', he must have had someone like Oscar in mind. Lao-tzu advised adults seeking virtue to 'manifest plainness, embrace simplicity, reduce selfishness, have few desires'. By these standards Oscar is there already. He is plain, simple, unselfish and undemanding. He is also supremely unconcerned about his own comfort. He speaks quietly and confidentially. His conversation is modest and never about himself. It consists entirely of pointing out interesting things such as cows, birds and motorbikes, either by naming them, or by parodying the noise that they make.

That other Chinese sage, Confucius, would have strongly approved of Oscar, too. The man of virtue, said Confucius, 'makes the difficulty to be overcome his first business, and success only a subsequent consideration'. This is Oscar all over when negotiating a steep flight of steps or stairs, for example, which is his chief difficulty at the moment. In his notable lack of prejudice, Oscar also conforms to Confucius' idea of the virtuous man not setting his mind 'either for anything, or against anything; he will follow what is right'. In short, the kind of company Oscar offers, once you've tuned in to it, is exemplary.

Of course I've heard incredible reports from his parents that Oscar is far from being the Confucian ideal when he's at home. That he hits his mother in the face, for example. That he whacks the baby. That he has tantrums. But I see none of it. From the moment he sees me he puts his best foot forward. It's as though he recognises a tribal elder when he sees one and knows how to behave.

At the open door of the public convenience, Oscar and I stood aside to make way for those coming out. There was variety in the men and boys exiting the public convenience. Each had a point of interest to commend him. This one was puffing at a cigarette. That one had excessive sideways motion and smelt of beer. This one looked like he wasn't used to crowded public conveniences and the experience had slightly traumatised him. Some offered us a mumbled apology. Oscar, too small to command attention, his small hand in mine, looked patiently up at the faces as they emerged one by one.

Finally an attractively unselfconscious, unafraid man emerged (thick gold chain necklace, tattooed hands), strenuously tugging the belt of his trousers up over his stomach with both hands. He looked me right in the eye, the first to do so, and when he looked down at Oscar his face shone with delight. He stopped in his tracks and stared in admiration. 'Little man!' he said in a voice steeped in phlegm and love. He said it to himself as much as to anyone else and he said it as if he couldn't help himself. And I'm not ashamed to say that his spontaneous approbation of our male child, from one tribal elder to another, exhilarated me.

After that I took Oscar on the dodgems. He was all set to drive when the lad keeping order came over and said sorry, gents, but it was against the rules.

DEAD BATS
24 October 2011

When my uncle was a boy, he said, he was leading a horse down a hill near North Weald in Essex. The horse was pulling a wagon loaded with cabbages, and my uncle had got down, he said, to assist the horse because the hill was a steep one. The war was on. The hill was on a quiet country lane, so he was surprised to see three limousines approaching together in convoy at speed. As the limousines drew level, they slowed to a walking pace so as not to frighten the horse. Seated in the back of the middle car, his face close to the window, and staring out, curious to see what was causing the delay, was Winston Churchill.

My uncle was nine or ten at the time, and he found himself staring directly into that famous, pugnacious face. The Prime Minister looked him in the eye, grinned and gave him the two-fingered V for victory salute. Then the car accelerated forward and he was gone.

My uncle told me this as we walked back to his smallholding from the nearest village, where we'd waited on the pavement, clutching our little sky-blue prostate cancer awareness flags, to see the Tour of Britain cycling race pass by. (If we'd blinked we'd have missed it.) That Churchill, even in an idle moment, and unobserved, would raise his game to rally the spirits of a small boy leading a horse in a country lane, added to his greatness in my eyes.

Wartime reminiscence continued back in the kitchen, where his elder sister was making herself a cup of tea. During the London Blitz, my grandfather moved his family from the relative safety and tranquillity of the countryside just outside London, into east London, to take advantage of the fall in property prices. Each night, as the family huddled in the Anderson shelter in the back garden listening to the falling bombs, my aunt, who is both fearless and intransigent, remained upstairs in her warm bed, sleeping peacefully. So we gave her the usual chaff about 'the woman who slept through the Blitz', which she takes in good part.

But my aunt does not take in good part statements or opinions with which she disagrees. Neither does my uncle. Nor did any visitor to their house during my stay or anyone else I met in Norfolk. I've never met such a disputatious set of people. They care nothing for civilised conversation. They prefer argument. Raise a subject, any subject at all, from the United States of America to the design of the pepper pot on the table, and there are only two possible ways of looking at it. It is either a good thing or it is a bad thing. It is right or it is wrong. And the only way to talk about something is to say you are in favour of it or to pour scorn on it. The Christian Church, Canada geese, the newsreader's tie, daisies, the Norfolk accent, automatic gearboxes, wind turbines: I was called upon to give each of these the thumbs-up or the thumbs-down, and my moral fibre and even perhaps my masculinity was judged according to my verdict. The only thing everyone could agree on wholeheartedly was capital punishment.

The argument about wind turbines rumbled on for three days. My uncle's wife says they are a good thing. My uncle's sister says they are a bad thing. She wants nuclear power. And just when I thought I'd finally heard the end of it, when we were gathered around the telly in a bucolic stupor, say, watching one of my uncle's DVDs about old Norfolk farming methods, the shouting match would begin again.

My uncle and his wife are well informed on the subject of wind turbines because one of their sons has three small ones on his farm. Also, their daughter and her husband have applied to have a big one on theirs, and as a consequence they have received death threats.

Inevitably, the wind turbine argument was reduced to one person insisting she liked them, and the other insisting she hated them. What did I think, they said? Terrified of being disloyal to either aunt, I said I thought they were a good thing as long as the revolving blades weren't dangerous to bats — a claim I've heard made by eminent bat people.

The next day we went over to my cousin's farm and everyone hobbled across the field to inspect his wind turbines. The blades were going like the clappers in the light breeze. I saw no dead bats, or dead anything, lying on the ground. Apparently, each turbine generated enough electricity to have a two-bar electric fire on permanently. 'Is that all?' scoffed my anti-wind turbine aunt. And the fatuously subjective argument was thus reignited and the two old bulldogs were at it again, even in the car on the way home.

SPIDER ON THE BUS
3 March 2012

At the moment we're very interested in spiders, my grandson and I. If we see one we catch it and put it in a clear plastic pot with a lid that doubles as a powerful magnifying glass, and we examine it. Last week we caught a monstrous one. It filled the pot. It was intelligent enough to quickly realise that escape was impossible and sat there looking thwarted. We took it in turns to squint at it through the magnifying lid. Oscar has no aesthetic sense as yet, and his powers of expression are very limited, yet he was visibly disconcerted by what he saw.

About once a week I take him on an outing. Lately we've gone somewhere and back on a bus because he loves buses with a passion. Suggested alternative outings are rejected out of hand. 'Train or bus?' I say. 'Bus.' 'Zoo or bus?' 'Bus.' 'Adventure park or bus?' 'Bus.' So we go on the bus.

We captured the spider on our bus-ride day, and I asked Oscar if he thought that the spider would like to come on the bus with us. He was certain that it would. We put a tragic poem of a dead and dried-up bumblebee in the pot with it in case it felt peckish on the journey. Also a live young woodlouse, which accepted the remarkable turn of events in its life with breathtaking insouciance.

On the bus we sat upstairs at the front as usual, with our insect gaol on the windowsill. The woodlouse was eagerly exploring the possibilities of the dead bumblebee. The spider clearly had a massive cob on.

At once Oscar and I began our usual exciting game of naming the things we saw as we went along. It seems absurd of the bus company to insist on putting on double-decker buses for a route through tortuous country lanes intended for donkey carts. But we are glad it does. Oscar has very keen eyesight and from the top of a double-decker bus can spot a cow grazing in a field two miles away. So far, we can name the following: car, van, truck, tractor, digger, gog (dog), bird, cow, sheep, goat, hen, sea, boat and mud. Our naming game can become repetitive, but Oscar's enthusiasm for the English language, with his particular liking for Anglo-Saxon words, normally sustains his grandad's flagging interest.

At the bus stop in the next village an elderly and familiar figure got on and came upstairs and sat behind us. As usual, Bill was dressed as if he was auditioning for Waiting for Godot and he smelt of sweat and ammonia. He is a lonely, sociable old man, and he leant his forearms companionably on the back of our seat to share our view. The smell was oppressive. And his patronising old countryman's assumption that we were entirely ignorant about the natural world was as irritating as usual. 'What have 'ee got in there, then?' he said, referring to the pot on the windowsill. I passed it over. 'Hallo. A spider. A big one,' he said authoritatively, adding: 'If you wish to live and thrive, let the spider run alive.'

And then the inevitable commentary on the surrounding countryside began. Every field and hedge is familiar to him. 'See this crossroads? That's where Mother used to wait for the bus on market day with 40 pound of butter strapped to her back. She'd already walked three mile to get here. In 'ot weather she was always so worried, God bless her, about it melting in the 'eat.'

'Gog,' said Oscar, annoyed by his dethronement and pointing to a dog on the beach. 'Yes, lovely gog,' I said.

'And see that woods over there on the hill?' said Bill. 'That's where Bert Pettigrew cut four of his toes off one day with a chainsaw. So he could stand nearer the bar, Father always used to say.' 'Cow,' said Oscar, referring to a miserable creature by a gate up to its knees in mud.

And so it went on. Two competing commentaries. Then, 'Bird!' said Oscar, pointing to a dense flock grazing in a waterlogged field. 'Rooks,' said Bill competitively. As one, the birds took off and wheeled low and obliquely across the field, revealing themselves to be not rooks at all, but lapwings. A magnificent sight. 'Lapwings!' said Bill. We three craned our heads to watch them. They were beautiful, thrilling to see. Oscar was pleased to have drawn our attention to them. Bill was pleased with his teacher's role in all of this. I was pleased simply to have seen them. For a moment we were a united, happy company, lurching from side to side high above the countryside. This was living. The woodlouse, eagerly exploring the corpse of the bumblebee, clearly felt the same way. Only the spider, hunched, introverted, had decided to sulk from start to finish.

JIMMY THE CAT
12 May 2012

The day after her 96th birthday, and three days before she died, my next-door neighbour told me she wanted her cat Jimmy killed and put in her coffin with her. Mrs Mee knew by then that she was dying and hadn't long to go. Was there anything I could do for her, I said? The only thing I could do for her now, she said, was put fresh milk in Jimmy's saucer, making sure that the milk was fresh. She was very anxious about this. She'd hate Jimmy to be offered milk that had gone off.

I came away jubilant. Mrs Mee wanting Jimmy put down was the best news I'd heard for ages. I'd have offered to do it myself with my bare hands if there was even half a chance she'd be amenable to the idea. From the moment Jimmy had turned up on her doorstep, half-starved, his once fluffy grey hair a tangled mat, she'd taken in and served this cat as if he were her sovereign. This otherwise sensible, frugal, vegetarian woman, who survived mainly on chips, fed this horrible cat on chicken breasts, organically reared ones if possible, as many as he could eat, and otherwise devoted her life to catering for his every whim. Far from appearing grateful, however, or humbled by his unexpected good fortune, Jimmy went about the place with the air of a spoiled and sulky child, and showed her not the slightest affection. She could tell that he understood that she was dying, she said, because he was acting 'huffily' and was more 'off' with her than usual. 'He knows, and he doesn't want anything to do with me now, the rotten beggar,' she panted.

On my way out, I noticed Jimmy glowering at me from the top of the stairs. He knew I detested him; that I was not impressed in the slightest by his regal bearing; that given half a chance I'd put a toe up his backside. And over the years he has paid me back handsomely for my disrespect. The ostentatious turd on the lawn. The trail of paw prints over the bonnet and windscreen of the car the day after I'd washed and polished it. The pitiful ring of blackbird feathers on the lawn marking the scene of a violent dismembering. He knew we cherished songbirds on our side of the wall. And he made sure that the sweeter the singer the more widespread the remains. An exuberant young thrush this year didn't last five minutes. Jimmy has always fled from me whenever I've had cause to go next door. On that particular day, however, it was as if he'd heard and understood he was going in the box, and couldn't contain his fury, and had to show it, albeit from the relative safety of the top of the stairs. As I passed beneath him, I looked up and waggled my eyebrows cheerfully at him.

Then Mrs Mee died, and her instruction to have the cat put down and arranged in the coffin was passed on to the next of kin. I made sure of it. Any doubt, I said, and I was willing to swear to it on the Bible. Not only that, I said, but I would also gladly save the vet the trouble by doing the job myself.

The vet was the preferred option. He could have refused to be complicit in the business on ethical grounds, apparently. But under all that luxuriant fur Jimmy had a tumour the size of a walnut on his head, and he was 14 years old, so the vet agreed to drive out and administer a lethal injection. The funeral director said he was happy to accommodate a dead cat in the coffin, but for a substantially increased fee. When it was pointed out to him that there was hardly anything of the owner left by the time she died, and that there would be room to spare in the coffin for another person, let alone a cat, he didn't press his case. It was agreed that he and the vet should come to the house at the same time, so that Jimmy would still be warm and more easily arranged in the coffin beside his faithful servant.

Jimmy was dozing on a chair when the vet arrived. He recognised the sound of the vet's car and possibly divined its significance. He instantly woke, flew upstairs, and resisted capture frantically, as if in full awareness that he was fighting for his life. A stealthier, better-armed attempt the next day failed before it had even begun, when Jimmy shot out through the door as the vet was let in.

Mrs Mee was eventually committed to the ground without Jimmy beside her. Jimmy is alive and now the sole occupant of Mrs Mee's substantial property. Yesterday I noticed him looking malevolently down at me from an upstairs window. Careful not to let him see how disappointed I am, I waggled my eyebrows cheerfully at him and gave him the wanker sign.

TWO HONEST COPPERS
11 August 2012

I was staying on Dartmoor at an old farmstead in an overgrown meadow next to a fast-flowing river. We built a fire by the river and sat around it on kitchen chairs drinking and talking. There was no phone signal, no radio, no internet, no telly, nothing. We didn't even have music. For two days and nights we heard only the sound of rushing water and sometimes wind in the trees. Wonderful it was to leave the tyrant iPhone on a windowsill to gather pollen and a cat's dusty paw print. I was so relaxed by the end I was horizontal.

On the third day, a Saturday, I'd promised to lend a hand at our village fête by doing a stint behind the bar. The organisers had said I should be there in the festive field for 12.30. But at 12.30 I was still sitting around the fire, a gin-and-tonic tray was circulating, and for some reason they tasted particularly wonderful that morning. They'll have plenty of help on hand at the fête, surely, was the cheerful consensus of opinion around the fire. 'Stay!' 'Have another!' 'Cheerioh!' 'The Queen!'

I stayed for one more, then another. Then my conscience got the better of me and I plucked my phone off the windowsill, tottered out to the car, and drove off the moor and down to my village at the coast.

After descending for eight miles my phone started pinging messages as I came back within range of the network signal. Steering the car with one thumb, I had a quick scroll through. One was from the police. This woman I'd met online and had known briefly had reported me as a missing person. She was extremely anxious about me, it said, and would I please contact them right away.

An explanation presented itself immediately. Because she never goes anywhere beyond the confines of the M25, she has absolutely no concept that parts of these islands have limited phone signal coverage, or none at all, and she must have worked herself up into a state. As I was late, I decided I'd drive on and contact the police when I'd arrived at the fête.

A happy throng was still pitchforking bales, shying balls at coconuts, and bowling for a piglet when I got there. A pair of policemen, one of whom I knew, added a vivid touch of fluorescent yellow to the scene. They spotted my entrance and made a beeline for me, intercepting me as I neared the barn where the bar was set up and where a number of the village big beasts were gathered. Could they have a word, said the policeman I knew?

The sun was shining hotly down on our happy village day; laughing children were running hither and thither; and here I was being taken aside for questioning. It might have been an intensely satisfying dénouement scene in an episode of Midsomer Murders. Kind, good people who assumed that I was as kind and as good as they, looked on half amused, half aghast. On reflection, I hadn't shaved for three days, and I was smoked like a kipper. My hair was standing up on end. My shoes were encrusted with river mud. Also, I was slightly tipsy. To a casual observer it might have appeared that I'd been missing for weeks, not days, and only the threat of death by starvation had driven me in from my hiding place on some remote crag.

The policeman I knew said that the woman who had reported me as missing had been particularly anxious because she'd interpreted my last text to her as a suicide note. Could he see it, please? I took out my phone, got the text up and showed him. It said: 'Clock that moon. Just risen. Driving. Anon.' I'd sent the text while driving up on to the moor, not imagining it would be my last contact with the outside world for some while. Neither I nor either of the two honest coppers could understand how she had interpreted this text as a suicide note. We shook our heads and rolled our eyes at one another at the mystery that is femaleness.

In fact my text seemed so far from being a suicide note that the copper I knew said perhaps I should also show them the previous text, in order to put it into some sort of a context. I scrolled back and returned my phone to the copper. He read it aloud for his colleague, who couldn't quite see. 'I need you to come and fill me up,' he read. 'I worship your body with all of my womanity.'

This made him blink four or five times. Then he looked beseechingly at his mate, as though they were perhaps the last two rational people left on this earth. 'With all of your what, darling?' said the other copper, leaning back in pretended horror.

WHO WANTS
MORE FANNY?
12 May 2012

We agreed that we ought to get dressed, leave the holiday apartment and do something else for a few hours in the evening. There was a choice. Richard lll performed outside on a grassy bank, or we could drive over to the St Ives School of Painting for the drop-in life drawing class. We had a copy of the play with us to acquaint ourselves with the plot. But while reading it she took offence at a misogynistic speech made by the hunchback King. Also the weather looked a bit uncertain. So the life drawing class it was.

She paints and draws and is familiar with life drawing classes. I'm used only to six-inch brushes and Dulux Weathershield. I'm not a prude — at least, not lately I'm not. Neither am I against public nudity. In fact, I live close to, and occasionally lie on, a popular nudist beach. But I wasn't sure that I wanted to scrutinise minutely a naked stranger from an embarrassingly short distance, then try to depict what I saw on a sheet of paper, then have my effort criticised by an art expert.

Knowing something of the history of the Porthmeor studios at the St Ives School of Painting (est. 1938), and of its famous alumni such as Terry Frost and Patrick Heron, I also expressed an anxiety that whoever was tutoring might resent having to lower themselves to comment on my toilet-wall-style of representation.

'Idiot,' she said.

We arrived a minute late. The studio was in a loft with a huge skylight and window views of Atlantic rollers breaking on the beach. It was exactly the kind of sexy, dusty, paint-spattered, cluttered, perhaps 1950s atmosphere I'd fondly expected. Faced with the reality, however, I cynically wondered whether it was artful design. As we walked in, four chaps and nine women were claiming pitches at an inward-facing circle of ancient wooden easels and contending for elbow room like a lot of territorial robins. In the centre of the circle was a dais covered with a blanket.

The tutor, a man, came forward and briskly told us to help ourselves to materials. It has been my (admittedly limited) experience of artists that anyone who dresses like an artist or talks like an artist probably isn't one. Proper artists, because of their neurotic illness, tend to go the opposite way and do their level best to blend in with the rest of us. This smart, casually dressed bloke might have been a modern civil servant. By my handy rule of thumb, I inferred from this that he was very possibly a painter of international repute. One or two of the older, grander, gaudier women in the room looked like artists from Hollywood central casting.

Informality was the keynote. We must help ourselves to paper, charcoal and bulldog clips, the tutor told us, and pay at the end by putting money in the tin. The largest sheets of paper cost 15 pence each, he said.

We found two easels together on the outer fringes. I was in her bad books straightaway for sharpening one of her pencils for her. One does not sharpen 4B drawing pencils, apparently. Then a young raven-haired woman in a blue towelling dressing-gown insinuated herself sideways through the crowding ring of easels and let the gown drop from her shoulders. She climbed lightly and confidently up on to the dais, lay on her side in a reclining pose that was somehow active rather than passive and which for all I know required skill. Her figure was voluptuous and her skin was nearly as white as my sheet of A2.

'Thank you, Sandra. Ten minutes,' said the tutor. Immediately everybody began scratching and scraping furiously at their paper sheets as though he'd let off a starting gun. My neighbour, one of the grander, gaudier women, noticed my incredulity at the speed and ferocity with which she was attacking the paper, and declared, 'Oh, I'm so ancient, darling, I can't possibly hang around waiting for inspiration.'

After ten minutes, Sandra changed position and orientation. After a further ten minutes, she changed again. This time, as she shifted position, she said, 'Who wants more fanny?' It was the only utterance I heard her make all evening. Nobody responded. They'd all gone into yet another concentrated frenzy of creativity.

Before the last pose before the tea break, I clipped a new sheet of paper to the easel, and when I looked up I saw that she was sitting on a small wooden chair right in front of me with her legs wide apart and she was looking me right in the eye. Going with her fanny joke, I held out my charcoal stick at arm's length, closed my left eye, cocked my head, and did that perspective measuring thing, with the charcoal tip on her aforementioned. She applauded with a lovely smile. 'Ten minutes!' said the tutor.

BEARDED LADY
13 October 2012

We hop on a bus. It's moderately full. We stand downstairs,
next to the doors. The bus pulls off and I study her from
the side without her noticing it. In a Sunday newspaper
style magazine that I read recently, there was a piece by a
woman writer about 'the ten things women really want
from a man'. These ten things were contrasted with the
'11 myths about what women want'. I read both lists
closely, having no idea either about the myth or the reality,
even at my age.

It is a myth, she claimed, for example, that women
like their men to take a serious interest in what they wear.
They don't, apparently. 'We want you to say, "That's new.
You look fantastic," not have an opinion,' she said.

We are at that early stage of a relationship where I
am astonished to see her wearing clothes, any kind of
clothes at all. And as the bus lurches and kangaroos
from one red light to another, I silently study hers
with the curiosity and wonder of an aboriginal from
an undiscovered tribe encountering a fully clothed
individual for the first time.

While the bus is briefly motionless at a bus stop, she
moves forward to consult with the driver about his route.
The driver answers conscientiously and at length, entailing
a small delay. The information he gives isn't clear to her,
and she asks for a restatement and clarification, which the
driver patiently supplies, extending the delay by perhaps a

further 10 to 15 seconds. She thanks him and makes her way back to the standing area.

Seated close to the front of the bus is this Valkyrie-type woman. Her heavy make-up and thick blonde plaits suggest a frantic fanning of the dying embers of her former youthful beauty. She's built like an ox. Seen from behind, the rigidity of her seated posture adds to the impression of a formidable determination allied to a fixed outlook.

As my new bird returns to her place in the standing area, the Valkyrie swivels her massive blonde head to the side and hisses an imprecation at her for the delay to our progress. The accent is Slavic.

The imprecation stops my new bird in her tracks. 'What!' she exclaims. She's amused at first, then astonished, then angry. 'How dare you!' she says to the Valkyrie. 'So you've been slightly delayed! And clearly such an important person, too! My God! Are you being met at the other end? Are they sending someone?' Then she takes a step back, to take in the whole, compared with which she is only about half the size. 'A forked lift truck, is it? And a specialist team of social workers?'

The Valkyrie cannot fully take in the depth of the rudeness at first. She yells back that she hasn't got all day to wait for people who don't know where they're going. 'Or are you a bearded lady in a circus?' adds my bird. 'And late for a performance?' Then she continues on back to the standing area, showing only the mildest signs of amusement at the encounter. It's not even significant or unusual enough for her to comment on. She's a tough one, all right. I can see I'm going to have my work cut out.

But the Valkyrie's determined mind has been dwelling on the comments directed at her. Now she's spitting feathers. She stands up and shouts, 'If you weren't such an old woman, I'd come back there and teach you a lesson.' A collective groan issues from the lower-deck passengers at this unexpected resumption of hostilities. 'And you'd do what, exactly?' my new bird replies.

I look at her. She's asking the question in a spirit of enquiry, good humour and hopefulness. She is utterly calm and composed. She is one of those exceptional people, clearly, whose minds, in the thick of a battle, become more tranquil, not less.

Another of the '11 myths about what women want' was that women like men to get into fights for them. 'No,' declared the writer. 'But there with the crushing put-down? Oh, yes, please.' But I get no sense, here, of being tacitly enlisted on her side. She doesn't need me. All the same, I prepare to get between them and push them apart. I have a mental image of a sticker given to me in my Sunday school days, of a sweaty Samson pushing apart the massive stone pillars of the Temple, with lumps of masonry falling all about him. 'So come on then!' she says, smiling eagerly at the Valkyrie. 'We haven't got all day, you know!'

I close my eyes and bow my head, lightly supporting my brow with the tips of my fingers. I'm currently going out with a warrior, it appears.

JUBILEE HAT
25 October 2012

Then she rented us a luxury apartment at Penzance in Cornwall for a week. Sightseeing was not high on our agenda. Bring cable ties, she'd said. I've been a naughty girl.

She went down by train; I drove. I drove due west for three hours through a rainstorm of tropical intensity. My new phone's blue light winked text messages from her all the way down. One said: 'Lost my musth. It's completely gone. Menopause?'

The apartment was called Stanhope Forbes, in homage to the leading light of the Victorian era Newlyn artists' colony. Stanhope Forbes's paintings of bustling late-Victorian fish quay scenes, with lovely girls in virginal pinafores, decorated the apartment's whitewashed walls. The domestic appliances were state of the art — I couldn't work out how to operate any of them — and the furniture was both contemporary and comfortable. Earlier in the week, she'd sent a photo of the lounge, excited about the possibilities offered by the low, comfortable-looking curves. With her musth now gone, at least the chances of her getting the damage deposit refunded in full at the end of the week had increased dramatically.

In case it stayed away, and we found ourselves with little or nothing to occupy ourselves, I applied for a week's temporary membership at the gym. Even though I'm a gym member at home, for health and safety reasons I would have to go through the long and tedious process of a three-part gym 'induction', warned the woman on the phone when I rang up. The splendid reality, however, was a friendly gym instructor looking me up and down, then saying, 'See that door there? That's the fire door. If there's a fire, you'll be following me out through it. Have a good workout.'

On the first day we visited St Ives. Middle England was there, possibly in its entirety, like a victorious army of occupation. We took refuge from the crowds in a small bookshop. After browsing for a while, I looked around and saw that she'd picked Fifty Shades of Grey off the shelf and was standing motionless as a statue, utterly engrossed.

'Listen to this rubbish!' she burst out. Then she read out a passage of dialogue. It was rather clichéd. I wandered about the shop fingering more paperbacks from the shelves. Another derisive snort from her and she read out a passage in which Anastasia receives a photograph from Christian, plus a message which says (something like): 'There are 30 surfaces in this picture. I want to have you on every one of them.' 'What crap!' she exclaimed. Then much less dogmatically, 'Isn't it?' Eventually I prised the novel from her hands, replaced it on the shelf and led her out of the shop.

The next morning, a Sunday, we went to church. Priest and congregation were blatantly Christian, and the incense lay so heavily in the air that it set her hay fever off. As we knelt at the altar rail to eat of the Body of Christ and drink of His Blood, she decided that she wouldn't or couldn't and she asked the priest to pray for her instead. Afterwards, walking down Market Jew Street, she spotted another interesting-looking bookshop. We went inside and she immediately made a beeline for Fifty Shades of Grey and began reading from where she'd left off in the other bookshop. My suggestion that I buy a copy was dismissed, however. 'It's just crap,' she said.

After that we went to the Penlee gallery at Penzance to see paintings by the Newlyn school, featuring an exhibition of paintings by Dame Laura Knight. The Newlyn school, I suppose, could be characterised as intensely realistic visions of rural pre-first world war innocence. No doubt the smart thing to do when confronted by the Newlyn school is to laugh. Personally, I'd have given anything to be allowed to step into one of those paintings and spend the remainder of my days living in that peculiar sunlight among those trusting faces.

'What do you think?' I said, inclining my head towards 'Jubilee Hat' by Frank Wright Bourdillon. The scene was a mother seated beside an open window, through which we were afforded a view of the bay. She has sewn a coloured ribbon on to the front of her best hat, in preparation for the Queen's Jubilee celebrations. She is holding the hat up to the light so her small son can also admire it. They are both keenly looking forward to the big day. The father is away with the fishing fleet, one imagines, but family and community life goes on.

She looked carefully at it for a long time. 'So did you bring those cable ties?' she said.

ADELSTROP
10 November 2012

I was on a train last Sunday evening, quite late. Reading in Berkshire to Redhill in Surrey, a journey of about an hour and a half. The train was three carriages long and we trundled at a leisurely pace across country, with frequent stops at freezing, deserted platforms. I was sitting in the front carriage with my back to the driver's cabin, on the left-hand side as you look forward. The driver and I must have been sitting back to back because I could hear him speaking on his phone now and again. I had the carriage to myself.

One of the stations near the end of the journey was called Dorking Deepdene. We were on time, perhaps even a bit early, because the driver eased his train very gently into the station and only the lightest of touches on the brake was needed to finally arrest the momentum. A second before the train came to a stop, however, with about ten feet to go, I felt the wheel directly under my seat ride over a bump. After about half a minute the driver's door opened, and I saw him walk past my window, flashing his torch into the darkness beneath the train.

At exactly the place where I'd felt the bump, I saw him kneel down on the platform and shine his beam carefully at something that interested him. Then I saw the train manager approaching from the rear of the train wearing a thick scarf wound around his neck for added protection against the freezing night. He had long black hair and a beard and he looked like a student. He had a torch, too, and he came and crouched beside the driver and shone it where the driver was shining his. Then the driver got to his feet with some difficulty because he was a big man and no longer young. Then he and the scholarly-looking train manager had a serious discussion.

The driver returned to his cab and I could hear him speaking on his phone again, but his voice was muffled by the partition and I couldn't hear what he was saying. And then the train's announcement system crackled into life and the young train manager's voice came on. 'Ladies and gentlemen, we apologise for the delay to this service, caused by an obstruction on the line here at this station. We are now waiting for the emergency services to attend. I will try to keep you informed of any further developments, but I can confidently predict that we will be remaining here for some time.'

And then he must have decided that there was little point in concealing from his passengers that we had all been obliquely involved in a terrible tragedy, because he concluded his announcement with: 'I can only repeat my apology for any inconvenience to your journey this evening, ladies and gentlemen, which is due to a fatality on the track.'

His announcement was followed by a long and deep silence. And then I could hear the driver speaking again on his phone on the other side of the partition. And then he, too, fell quiet. My carriage was so silent I could hear myself breathing. I looked out of the window. The platform was silent, deserted. Nobody came or went. It was Adlestrop for the 21st century.

I stood up and went to the carriage door and pressed

the lit 'open' symbol. The door hissed, sighed, opened. At the same moment the young train manager appeared in the vestibule and we stepped out and down on to the platform together. 'Can I see?' I said. He saw no reason why I shouldn't. Like an impresario, though a faintly embarrassed one, he gestured with an arm that all I had to do was look down.

Yellow platform light penetrated the gap between the platform edge and the carriage, illuminating the large jacketed torso of a man. The jacket was a desirable new Belstaff, and it was comprehensively belted and zippered against the cold. He had laid on his back and placed the back of his neck on the rail. The train had entered the station so slowly he must have been crouching in the shadows just beneath the platform and picked his moment nicely. The wheel rested on his neck obscured the fact of whether his head was severed from his body or not. Bright arterial blood was sprayed about ten feet up the line.

I stood and looked at the train manager. He was calm but appropriately sad. I think he was a Spaniard. He said, 'I can't believe that's a dead body down there.' 'Surely you get them all the time,' I said. 'My first,' he said. 'In four and a half years.' Then he walked away towards the front of the train and climbed in beside the driver to wait with him for the emergency services.

ASIA VS AFRICA
17 November 2012

Two policemen and a policewoman were the first of the emergency services to arrive on the platform. The policemen ran about like headless chickens. The woman was calmer. She quickly grasped the essentials of the situation, such as under which wheel the suicide lay, and who had been driving the train.

Then more police arrived, and a paramedic team. One of the paramedics knelt down, then got his head and shoulders under the carriage and reached down and felt the dead man's wrist for a pulse. Then the policewoman, noticing that there were passengers still on the train, indignantly ordered the train manager to evacuate it.

This he did, netting around a dozen of us. He shepherded us down two flights of metal steps and told us to wait there, at the foot of the embankment. Typically, perhaps, for a random cross-section of the travelling public taken late on a Sunday night, we were a motley crowd. Most noticeable among us was a pair of teenage lovers who couldn't keep their hands off one another; a gentle, ruddy-faced giant roused from sleep with his hair sticking up; a Pre-Raphaelite beauty placidly texting on her iPhone; and an obese woman with purple lipstick proclaiming her African heritage with an ankle-length cotton dress and multicoloured shawl.

Ten minutes later, the train manager returned. We gathered round him, eager for information. More than likely a bus would be sent to pick us up and take us to our final destinations, he said, but exactly when this bus might arrive he couldn't yet say. He appreciated that it was a freezing night, but he hoped we would all be on our way again soon. Nobody asked him a question about the 'fatality'. Whether this was out of politeness or a terrible lack of curiosity, I couldn't say. Someone wondered aloud whether we weren't few enough to warrant a taxi each. The train manager said he'd ask.

It was indeed very cold standing about. You could almost hear the temperature plummeting, like a high-pitched tinnitus. Already the dead yellow and orange leaves at our feet glistened with frost. I burrowed my chin into my collar. More members of the emergency services were arriving: a doctor, a rail company accident and investigation team; more paramedics; more police. They came striding up the asphalt path head to foot in bright yellow. We had to step aside to make room for them to pass. It was noticeable how far we were beneath their notice. Not a single one had the largeness of spirit to offer as much as a friendly nod. They all kept their heads down and barged past, taking it for granted that once we'd registered a fluorescent yellow jacket approaching, we'd briskly step aside.

And all of them on double time, too, I'll wager. Finally there must have been 30 members of the emergency services milling about up there on the platform, enjoying themselves. The pious thought occurred to me that it was a pity that a similar abundance of resources and attention wasn't lavished on the man before he laid his neck on the rail, instead of afterwards.

After about half an hour, the train manager appeared among us again. We gathered frozenly around, avid for news. A bus had just left London, he reported, and would be here within the hour. The teenage lovers slipped back into the shadows and lit up another fag each. The Pre-Raphaelite beauty went back to her texting. The ruddy-faced giant ran a huge, tired hand over his unruly hair. The woman with the colourful shawl, however, took this news very badly. Her broad face disintegrated into a series of lines and creases and she threw back her head and wailed like a baby, with long shuddering intakes of breath in between. She gave it everything she had. Then she yelled, 'I'm tired! I'm cold! I'm sick! I want a taxi! And I want one right now!"

We eyed her with horror. Someone had just been decapitated under our train. Surely this was no time to be complaining about having to wait for a bus. But she was only saying what we were all thinking. We were bloody freezing standing there. Was anyone else going to side with this woman, to clamour for special treatment, I wondered?

"You are a very ignorant, selfish woman," piped up a petit Asian lady who was standing quietly on her own. "And would you please shut up."

Any waverers resolve now stiffened by the moral decisiveness of the Asian lady, we watched the big African woman's mental collapse with a mixture of pity and disgust. But it had been a close run thing.

VALPOLICELLA
AND POINSETTIAS
31 December 2012

I was standing on the pavement outside the Lahore Kebab House, Hendon, after a three-hour lunch, waiting for a minicab. Fifty of us had sat down at a flower-laden table to samosas and champagne, kebabs and Valpolicella. Amid a convivial uproar, our host had stood, tapped his water glass with his spoon, and made a speech of thanks and welcome. Last year, to our host's transparent consternation, his speech was hijacked by Lord Charles, the ventriloquist's dummy, who'd made obscene remarks about some of the guests. Today his speech was again persistently interrupted, this time by Sooty on the one hand, and by Sweep on the other, whispering irrelevant comments in his ear. At this early stage I was sitting next to an endlessly interesting Scot who'd started out in life playing left back for St Mirren. The Valpolicella was out of this world, it dawned on me after about the third glass.

A biting wind was blowing up the high street and no sign of a minicab anywhere. I didn't know, and I didn't much care, what I was going to do next, or where I should go, or even what was to become of me, so it didn't much matter. Then two women bearing poinsettias came out. They were hoping for a minicab also, they said, leaning tipsily together for mutual support. What about we share the next minicab that came along, they said, and go back to their place for a party? Both were blonde and slender under their long winter coats and they exuded a pleasant kind of recklessness. Good idea, I said.

Next, a racehorse trainer whom I hadn't noticed at the lunch, but recognised from off the telly, came out, also in search of a minicab. I think he might have had a few, too. He was heading south, he said. 'Come back to our place!' chorused the tipsy blondes. The racehorse trainer's cheerful face became momentarily downcast, even slightly bitter. He couldn't, unfortunately, he said. The tipsy blondes lolled back their heads and wailed in sulky disappointment.

Then a smart gent with a tweed overcoat and expensive glasses came out and offered his cigarettes around, as if the more people who took one, the happier it would make him. He presented the packet of Lucky Strikes with both hands, humbly, imploringly, as though it really was his supreme privilege to be able to offer something that everybody wanted. He'd have given the entire packet away if he could have found enough takers. I hadn't seen that oriental-like combination of generosity and humility, I thought, for many years.

Then a minicab pulled up and the pair of tipsy blondes, the cheerful racehorse trainer, the generous smoker and I got in and settled ourselves among the poinsettias. Unfortunately, we had to evacuate immediately because the minicab turned out to be for someone else.

Two seconds later another minicab arrived and the driver of this one gravely indicated that he was at our service. We bundled in, again carefully settling the poinsettias between us. The racehorse trainer volunteered to sit in the boot. I sat in the front passenger seat. As we nosed forward into the slow traffic, the racehorse trainer made a complaint to the driver about a nasty smell in the boot. Then he embarked on this comic shtick, in the form of a bitter soliloquy, about what a fastidious man he is, and how sensitive he is to nasty smells. The generous smoker produced an opened and almost full bottle of Valpolicella from the depths of his overcoat and eagerly passed it around. When it was the driver's turn, he politely and regretfully shook his head.

United now by our little comedy of errors, by the cigarettes, by the cosy warmth of the cab, by our southward direction of travel, by our shared concern for the poinsettias' well-being, by the racehorse trainer's running commentary on the smell, by the circulating bottle of Valpolicella, by Lionel Richie singing 'Say You, Say Me' on the radio and, united above all by that camaraderie to be found among inebriate flotsam everywhere, we began singing, together with Lionel, the chorus of 'Say You, Say Me'.

Even the racehorse trainer briefly forgot about the smell and his voice could be heard from the back, blending plangently with ours. And as we sang, I looked around in the darkness at the sporadically illuminated faces, and I was overcome with love for every one of us, even for myself. For we had arrived at a pitch of harmonious understanding, it seemed to me, that I hadn't thought humanly possible, least of all in any sort of company with me in it, and I wanted us all to live together in a commune planted with poinsettias, the minicab driver also, and we'd all drink Valpolicella, and be this well dressed, and this well fed, and sing together like this, for the rest of our days.

DR MUK
26 January 2013

Dr Muk asked me whether I'd heard any more news about the Syrian hostage crisis. Had the number of hostages killed been announced yet, for example? 'I simply don't understand these Islamist terrorists,' he added, sadly. 'They seem absolutely crazy to me. They are brainwashed, I suppose.' I hadn't listened to the radio so far today, I said, so I wasn't up to date. But if you asked me, I said, they quite possibly have a point. Maybe our secular, materialist society is as contemptible as they claim it is. 'Mm. Mm,' agreed Dr Muk with surprising readiness.

I was lying on my back and he was slicing open my upper chest with a scalpel. The local area was anaesthetised, so I couldn't feel a thing. The last time I was under his knife, six months ago, he'd failed to remove the corruption entirely. He'd missed a bit. So here I was again and he was unzipping the scars and ranging wider and deeper with his sharp instruments.

Dr Muk was leaning over me from the right-hand side; his assistant was leaning over me from the left. Half of his assistant's face was covered by a mask, and she wore glasses, but behind the glasses her blue eyes were wonderfully expressive. She communicated friendliness, reassurance and good humour easily with them. I felt like a child in a cradle being doted on by loving parents.

Dr Muk's real name is Mukopadhyay, but to his operating team here in Devon he's Dr Muk. He is a slightly built and

65

very gentle, otherworldly man. I feel at a slight disadvantage in his company, given that our entire acquaintance has consisted of my lying underneath him with my chest bared, and him knifing me, but his delicacy and modesty is such that it is always I who have the impression of being the one deferred to.

The unmistakable sound of the Hammond organ introduction to 'A Whiter Shade of Pale' by Procol Harum began playing in the background on the CD player. One of the nurses went over and turned up the volume and sang along to the chorus. 'Oh, God. She's off,' said Steve, whose job as acting quartermaster is to pass out the dressings as and when required. 'She's cycling across Cuba next month, aren't you, Val?' he said. 'For charity. She's going topless.'

Val's job is to write down certain phrases dictated to her by Dr Muk. Phrases like 'lesion, right clavicle' and 'left anterior chest'. 'They've told us we've got to concentrate on the road all the time because of the potholes, so we won't be seeing much of the countryside, unfortunately,' she admitted. Then she started singing along to the chorus of 'Whiter Shade of Pale' again and Steve clapped his hands over his ears.

'Don't you like Procol Harum, then, Steve?' I said, turning my head to look at him. Steve is about 60 years old. 'I prefer modern stuff,' he said. 'Garage?' I said. 'Yes, I like some garage,' he said with dignity. 'Ever taken an e?' I said. 'He's done everything, Steve has,' warned Val. 'Haven't you, Steve?' 'Yes, I have taken one, actually,' said Steve, quietly proud. 'Once. At a Conservative club. I didn't notice any effect because I was drunk. We'd been on a coach tour of all the Conservative clubs in the area and this bloke got some out and handed them round for a laugh.'

I knew what he meant, I said, because exactly the same thing happened to me the only time I ever smoked heroin. I was so drunk I didn't notice any effect whatsoever. 'Was that in a Conservative club as well?' said Val. 'No, in a mental hospital,' I said. 'But there can be no justification for such brutality, even as a means of expressing disagreement,' said Dr Muk. I looked up at his face. His concentration was on his surgical incisions, his expression was one of gentleness and competence. But a part of his mind dwelt still on those Islamic militants.

'Perhaps they think it's the only language that hypocrites like us are likely to fully understand,' I said.

'Hypocrites?' exclaimed Dr Muk's assistant. 'Us? What about them? They're the biggest hypocrites of the lot! What about them and alcohol? And sex!' She wasn't having any more of my nonsense and swabbed at the blood coming out of my chest with considerably more vigour than she had done hitherto. 'Mm. Mm,' agreed Dr Muk.

Another chorus of 'Whiter Shade of Pale' came around again — the final one — and Val joined in, with feeling. Steve clapped his hands over his ears and retreated over to the wall. Dr Muk paused briefly to adjust his magnifiers, and then bent to his task again with renewed concentration.

BUTLINS!
4 May 2013

I've lately got into the habit of starting off a Saturday night out in a quiet pub at the top of the town. I like the draught Japanese lager and the ridiculous glasses it comes in. The pub is friendly enough, but I don't get involved. I have two or three pints, nod thanks, and move on. But the last time I was in there, one of the regulars said did I want to go to a music festival at Butlins in Minehead next weekend? A crowd of them were going. Twenty bands. Blockheads, Bad Manners, Selector. Come; it'll be a laugh, he said.

I arrived in the early evening of the festival's second day. At the check-in counter, I was delighted to learn that I had been upgraded from a room only to an apartment. But where were my new pals? And how would I find them? I knew none of their surnames. Butlins at Minehead is the size of a small town. I had the phone number stored of the chap who'd invited me, but my phone was away at the menders.

The lads in the next apartment to mine were sitting out on the balcony playing a drinking game involving a plastic funnel and four feet of tubing. They were dressed as jockeys in yellow and mauve quartered silks. I made myself a nice cup of tea, then went for a wander around the site. On the footpaths between the rows of apartments and chalets, I encountered punks, mods, bikers and gangs of blokes dressed in bondage and fetish gear, or dressed as sexy nuns in fishnet stockings and suspenders, or as Playboy bunnies. Cross-dressing seemed to be the ultimate party statement. Most people were boozing inside their chalets or seated outside on plastic chairs enjoying the evening sunshine. I wasn't stared at, but I felt self-conscious. I must have been the only straight, stone-cold sober, boringly dressed person on the site. And this slightly paranoid consciousness of not being in the swim was accentuated a few minutes later when I ran into my new pals, who were standing around a table outside one of the bars.

They were in the swim alright. They were all completely off their faces. I hardly recognised them as the sedate regulars I knew from the quiet, rather intellectual pub. It was perhaps a miracle that they recognised me. Beyond effusive, inarticulate greetings, I couldn't get any sense out of any of them, apart from, 'It's fantastic!' Or, 'It's just fantastic!' Or, 'It's really, really fantastic!' I turned from one to the other hoping to move the conversation on, but they seemed to have been seized by a collective delirium. One or two couldn't even speak at all. Others were jabbering away 15 to the dozen but not rationally. It was as though against all expectations they'd come to Butlins at Minehead, stumbled on the secret of happiness, and gone mad at the same instant.

I was pleased for them; jealous even. Added now to my sense of coming late to the party, however, was the realisation that I wasn't in a party mood. I went to the bar to buy a pint, thinking I might try to catch up. It did no good. My thoughts turned to my nice apartment. I'd brought daffodils to make it homely and books and tins of soup. I made a decision to have a night in. Without taking my leave of my new pals, I returned there (the jockeys were gone), sat down on a sofa and opened a book — a 1935 Hogarth Press edition of The Common Reader by Virginia Woolf – and started reading the first essay, 'The Pastons and Chaucer'.

I've never read any of Virginia Woolf's novels with as much enjoyment as I read this essay. I was utterly enthralled and amazed by the quality of the writing and the clear-sightedness of her historical perspective. I read it in a kind of rapture, dreading coming to the end while still at the beginning. It was just fantastic. That I had my reading head on had a lot to do with it. I was in the right mood, both for her and her subject. But was it more than that? This unexpected and normally temporary deepening of enjoyment of the English language has happened to me abroad sometimes. Somehow English becomes more vivid to this native speaker when read in countries where it isn't widely spoken. Is a like, mysterious process at work at Butlins, Minehead? Does Butlins, with its long experience, understand what makes you happiest, whatever it is, then deliver it without further ado? I read 'The Pastons and Chaucer' by Virginia Woolf twice through, savouring every sentence, dimly conscious that the caterwauling of the revellers passing the window, and the wailing of the seagulls copulating clumsily on the roof opposite, were becoming ever more raucous.

DAY RETURN
TO WATCHET
11 May 2013

Next morning, Sunday, up early. I must have been the only person at the Butlins music festival minus a hangover. Day three, and I was yet to hear a live musical note or get myself an altered consciousness. I walked into town along the promenade feeling ever so noble. Perhaps I might go to church, I thought, and underline my great goodness. I savoured an image of my new pals, hands on hips, indignantly saying to me, 'So where were you last night?' And my answering, 'I had an early night.' And them saying, 'And today? Where were you today?' And me saying simply, 'Church.'

The sea was flat and grey. Other festival-goers, cold and crapulent, were slouching grimly into town, as though on a forced march. The promenade ran out near a quaint old railway station. I was surprised to see one. I'd imagined that the hills of Exmoor were a barrier to every line of communication except the unbelievably stoney, winding road that had brought me here.

I crossed the road to see if it was still functioning. The booking office was a homely, pre-Beeching affair, smelling of fresh paint and coal smoke. A loud whistle. A train was about to leave. A steam train. 'Don't worry about a ticket,' said a man in a peaked cap with an unguarded, unhurried, perhaps pre-Beeching air. 'Buy one on the train. No need to hurry!' he called after me, as I broke into an anxious trot past the second-hand bookstall.

I climbed aboard and passed through the train as far as the buffet. The carriages smelled of dust and smoke. The few passengers on either side seemed to be of a type: mild, elderly, quietly ecstatic. The buffet was a fully stocked bar, with upside-down gin, vodka and whisky bottles, big ones, on prominently displayed optics. The counter was manned by a woman who looked as if she'd seen everything. I was terribly tempted by these magnificent spirit bottles, but it was 10.15 a.m., and I'm not Nigel Farage, peace be upon him.

I chose coffee and asked her where we were going. Bishops Lydeard, she said, an hour and a quarter away, with eight stops in between. I asked her whether she had any suggestions as to where I might get off. 'Watchet's nice,' she said. So I went there.

Watchet, it turned out, is a tiny, ancient fishing port shielded from the outside world by the Quantock hills. The train stopped next to the harbour. I stepped down into dazzling sunlight and the crying of gulls. A noticeable absence of motor vehicles and the calmness of a quiet Sunday morning added to my strong impression of going further and further back in time. Thirty yards from the station was a tourist information office in what must once have been a fisherman's cottage. The door was open. The man inside was standing among the racks of brochures and leaflets rolling a fag. He betrayed no emotion when I asked him about the times of the church services in Watchet. There was a handy ecumenical leaflet. Quickly scanning it, I saw I'd missed them all.

'Where can I get a drink, then?' I said, caving in suddenly. He led me outside and pointed to the doorway of a club not 20 yards away. 'In there's not bad,' he said.

'You'll have to sign the visitors' book. It opens at 12.' He raised a flame to his fag and I got out one of mine and accepted his light. It was a peaceful, sunny spot and very pleasant to be standing there with this non-judgmental tourist information officer, smoking, chatting in a desultory manner, and gazing out over the sea at the opposite shore. I asked a further question, about whether Watchet was the Matchet of Evelyn Waugh's Men at Arms. He knew the book. He knew it well. But he rather thought not. We smoked on. Then, risking losing what little confidence in my intelligence that he might have had, I said, 'And what is that coastline over there? Is it Wales?' I was quite correct, he said. Wales.

And then I went and ate ham, egg and chips in a tearoom that reminded me strongly of the one in Walmington-on-Sea where Captain Mainwaring goes for his lunch. And then I went to the little museum and put a quid in the wooden box beside the door. And by then it was midday. I went to the club, signed myself in, and got deliberately and totally drunk. I missed every train back to Butlins but the last. I went again to the buffet. 'How was Watchet?' said the woman behind the counter. 'Fantashtic!' I said. When I got back to the festival, however, and rejoined my new pals, they were having such a lovely time that I don't think I was even missed.

THAI BRIDES
20 May 2013

On Sunday morning early I was trying to hitch a ride home. A big white Mercedes van came haring around the bend. I stuck out my thumb and it swerved violently and stopped beside me. 'A good night, then, was it?' said the driver as I collapsed into the passenger seat. A comedian. Young fella. Wide awake. Chewing gum. Loving the life. It must have been my glassy eyes and my crumpled, slept-in jacket that gave me away. I had a think. Not bad, I said. I listed the names of the pubs and the two clubs we'd been to. 'So did you pull?' he said.

Pardon? I said. 'Pull. Last night. Did you get hold of anything?' he said. It's true, I told him, that it would have been nice not to have frozen half to death in the foetal position on a pal's tiny sofa with a tea towel for a duvet, and been invited instead into a warm and spacious bed. But as usual I was not an attractive proposition as a prize to be carried off into the night for a one-night stand. So no, I said. I didn't pull.

He shot me this look of a disappointed mentor. I'd badly let him down. 'There were a few spares knocking about though, surely?' he said, needing to understand fully and allow for any mitigating circumstances. There were indeed a good many 'spares', I said, thinking back. Especially at the clubs. You couldn't move for them. We hadn't seen anything like it for a long time. I was often the only bloke on a dance floor packed out as far as the eye could see with groups of grooving ladies. I was moving from one group to the next to give as many as possible the benefit of seeing my moves at close hand, I said.

His lively face was turned avidly towards mine more often than it was towards the road ahead. 'And?' he said. 'You're telling me you didn't score?' 'It didn't even occur to me to try,' I said. 'I was so drunk I couldn't speak, one. Two, I've never been one for charades. And three, they were laughing at me, as if to say, "Look out, sisters, here comes the oldest swinger in town — and just look at the state of it!"'

He was powering his tall van through the lanes, leaning his body into the curves, really driving the thing. But on hearing this, he slumped wearily forward, rested both elbows on his steering wheel, and shook his head in despair, Then he revived himself just in time to take a sharp right-hander. Like I say, a comedian. After that he brooded and we rattled along without speaking. 'You should go to Thailand,' he said finally. 'The birds are different over there.' 'Different?' I said. 'How's that?' 'Ever been?' he said. I shook my head. 'Oh, mate,' he said, anguished.

Then he fell silent again, momentarily lost in a private fantasy. His Thailand experiences were obviously so rich and varied he hardly knew where to begin. Nor could he quite put his finger on that particular aspect of Thai women that made them so very different from our English ones. 'They're just different, that's all,' he explained. 'They don't muck about.' And they don't cost much? I said, happy to show I was not entirely ignorant about the subject. 'Yeah, yeah, you buy them,' he said. 'Where don't you? But I don't mean that. What I mean is. Here.'

He reached out for his iPhone and driving with one hand he pulled up his camera roll and flicked through it with his thumb. Then he leaned across and showed me a picture of very young loveliness smiling warmly and openly for the camera. 'I bought that one off her parents last year for 15 hundred quid. Nice boobs, eh?' he said. There was absolutely no denying it. 'I had those put in,' he said. 'Five hundred quid the pair. What a little darling. She adores me.'

'That's quite an investment,' I said. 'Do you think you'll marry her? Get an import licence and have her crated up and forwarded? Here you go, this is me,' I added, for we'd arrived already at the turning where I got out. He slammed on the anchors. As I searched for the door handle, I noticed that he was now looking at me with a new, almost pleading seriousness that wasn't nearly as becoming as his previous archness. I thought at first it was a variation on his comedian's repertoire, but it wasn't: I must have touched a nerve. 'Do you know what, mate?' he said. I braced myself for his big confession. 'It's something to think about.' I jumped out, slammed the door and set off down the lane. I felt terrible, really terrible.

ZOO TRAIN
27 May 2013

The train driver was at lunch. The next train to depart, according to her blackboard, was 13.00. It was now 12.45. The miniature diesel locomotive and the row of blue carriages were empty in the station. Shut in his house on the far side of the lake, the lion, deeply troubled, was roaring his head off.

My grandson chose a carriage two from the front. He insisted on being the one who turned the little brass knob that opened the low door. The zoo train's carriages are open carriages with room for two passengers, one facing forward, one back, knees touching. Our ice creams were starting to melt and drip. I found a paper serviette in my pocket and wiped the ice cream from his chin and hands and then I licked his lopsided ice cream back into shape and returned it. Alone on our beloved zoo train, we sat and finished our ice creams in perfect accord.

We'd had a marvellous morning. We'd seen tigers, we'd seen lions, we'd seen a matamata. (The matamata was standing glumly in exactly the same place in its tank of brown opaque water as it was the last time we came.) We'd seen the new orangutan baby that was featured on the local television news. We'd seen a huge mountain gorilla swing over and thump the safety glass so violently and unexpectedly with his forearm that a woman with a pushchair had screamed hysterically and made everyone, even herself, laugh.

Oscar had literally jumped for joy when I'd picked him up earlier that morning. He jumped up and down twice, an arm reaching for the sky. I don't think anybody has jumped for joy to see me before. A good part of his joy, though, I expect, was inspired by the expectation of a ride on the zoo train. And now that wonderful prospect was nearly a reality. In ten minutes' time the driver would return from lunch, contort herself into the driver's cabin, toot the whistle, and our happiness would be complete.

More passengers arrived: a mother and father with two girls. They scrutinised the time chalked on the blackboard and compared it with that shown by their own and each other's watches. Mother and father (especially father) were remarkably fat, even by the standards of the day. They looked at the row of waiting carriages and at us sat there licking our ice creams.

Father was wearing a Bridgend rugby shirt. He lit a tailor-made cigarette and puffed it furtively. Mother sank down on to a wooden bench. Their two girls swarmed delightedly into the front carriage from where they taunted their father about his great fatness. He will be able to fit his arse on to a carriage seat only with the greatest difficulty, they predicted. Father accepted this with a sheepish look and another furtive puff.

The friendly Welsh, God bless them. But we were in unfriendly England. As much as I would have liked to have offered them a welcoming 'Afternoon!' or 'All aboard!' I abstained. Unless you are having a manic episode you can't go to the zoo in England and greet absolutely everyone who catches your eye. So I said nothing. I sat there instead with as much self-containment as it is possible for an adult to have sitting on a toy train licking an ice cream. I did, however, do a friendly eyebrow waggle over my ice cream at the girls to indicate that we in our carriage were in a quietly celebratory mood, and therefore they must feel free to misbehave and insult their father as much as they liked.

Father finished his cigarette and discreetly disposed of the end. Surely he wasn't really going to attempt to squeeze himself into a carriage seat, was he? He was. He ambled over to the train, stooped to turn the tiny brass knob on one of the carriage doors and climbed in. His girls went wild with hilarity. He aligned his vast bulk above the seat and gingerly lowered himself into place. It was an agonising squeeze, but he made it, in spite of his person being wider physically than the carriage. The girls said he would never be able to get his fat arse out again and that he would have to go round and round on the train all afternoon. Father looked dispiritedly resigned to the fact.

Then — blessed moment! — the train driver returned from her lunch break and collected all the tickets. More passengers filled the carriages. And at one o'clock precisely, she inveigled herself into the driver's cabin of the locomotive and let go a long shrill blast on the whistle. 'Here we go!' shouted Oscar, his disconcerting pellucid eyes wide with joy. From across the lake, the lion roared out his disgruntlement.

DOGGIES!
1 June 2013

On bank holiday Monday my brother and I, and my brother's three Border terriers, went for a day-long walk on Dartmoor. We weren't the only ones up there. And I often wonder whether the hardy, reclusive souls who live up there, having endured another long winter, aren't a little peeved to find their peace shattered by the walkers, cyclists and day trippers who swarm all over the place at the first sign of spring.

But to our credit, we at least looked the part. Clown that I am, I was head to foot in lightweight, quick-drying walking clobber, my suede walking shoes made in Germany, and on my back a snug-fitting, 15-litre daysack. The day before I'd sat in a busy barber's chair and told him to give me whatever it was that the kids who wear their hair short are asking for these days. They are asking for a 'Hitler Youth' apparently, and five minutes later I emerged from his shop with closely shorn back and sides and a ruler-straight parting. So I was every inch the pre-war Wandervogel.

My brother wore walking boots, but otherwise doesn't need specialist gear to look the part. He is a strapping, rugby-playing policeman and judo black belt with biceps bigger and rounder than my calves. Next month he's off to Northern Ireland to earn some of the £50 million that the security operation for the rash G8 summit is going to cost us. One day last week police instructors threw petrol bombs at him all afternoon.

I must mention the dogs, too. My brother had stripped out their winter coats and they looked as lithe and lean as racing snakes, and a credit to the breed, though if there was any well-rotted cow manure lying about, Ruby in particular wolfed down as much as she could before my brother noticed and started yelling.

As I say, man and dog we looked the part: fit to tackle the steepest gradient or the most difficult, rock-strewn country. The focus of our walk was Lustleigh Cleave, which is basically a gash in the landscape with a rushing river at the bottom and splendid views to be had from the high plateau on the eastern side. At the northern end of this plateau are the remains of an Iron Age fort, one of a chain from which local tribes are said to have stood and faced the Romans. Coins found in the vicinity showing a gormless, laurel-wreathed profile of the emperor Hadrian suggest that here as elsewhere the challenge was vigorously met and the defenders annihilated.

We ascended to the ridge by the northern slope. The path was long, tortuous, stony and steep. We passed close by a group of Belted Galloway cattle lying in the shade of a massive granite boulder. Their great black eyes swivelled in their heads as they tracked the terriers' activity. The going was tough. Even my brother was panting. Droplets of sweat stood out on his brow. I tripped, stumbled, regained my balance, tripped, stumbled again.

Finally, we passed through a gate on to the bright and airy spaciousness of the plateau. Conveniently close by was the heap of granite boulders known as Hunters Tor. We sat on this and sipped coffee and looked down at the panorama of magnificent countryside laid out before us. A peculiarly rich and enchanting silence reigned, interrupted occasionally by the articulate bleating of a distant sheep, now distinct, now muffled by a passing breeze, now distinct again. Up there on the plateau were the usual strangenesses one encounters on Dartmoor: the boneyard litter; the sparkle of rock crystals; the wind-warped, lichen-bearded trees; the house-sized boulders; the strange ants, parti-coloured, radiating intelligence. All this was our reward for our effort.

Then we saw, coming steadily towards us across the uneven ramparts of the Iron Age fort, this nerdy-looking young bloke, designer glasses, trendy short-leg chinos, Birkenstock sandals, pushing a baby-buggy with a slumbering child in it. 'Hi!' he said gaily, as he drew near. Following behind was a heavily pregnant, palpably serene woman, pretty dress, also in sandals, with a flower in her hair, holding a cheerful little girl by the hand. 'Hi!' she said, languidly. 'Doggies!' said the little girl, excitedly pointing.

They didn't seem remotely out of breath or animated by their arduous ascent. I studied the map to find the nearby car park I must have missed. There wasn't a road anywhere near us. The path by which they had ascended, and by which we now began our descent, was, we found, if anything steeper and trickier than the one we had laboured up. There was no other route. As we staggered and stumbled down the rocky path, my brother and I laughed and laughed in awe and wonder at that laid-back couple; also with relief, perhaps, at the quality of the rising class and generation they represented.

LEEKY LEEKS
8 June 2013

Three miles up the road is a glass-fronted cupboard in a hedge that often contains free-range eggs for sale at £1.20 a half-dozen. It's a sales point relying on and trusting in other people's honesty. You slide back the glass, pleased to be living in a still-civilised part of the world, drop your coins in the tin and help yourself. The eggs are flecked with dirt and crap and bits of straw, and one of these boiled for three minutes and eaten with a slice of bread and butter is what I'd ask for if I ever find myself on Death Row on the morning of my execution.

Recently I've discovered another honesty stall consisting of a rickety table outside a thatched cottage in an unfrequented lane. This one offers garden vegetables, and I've become a regular customer here, too. The egg cabinet I pass most days in the car. The vegetable table, however, is not on a route to anywhere, so I've incorporated it into a five-mile circular walk as a highlight, and I visit there once or twice a week. I'm leading a fairly quiet life at the moment (if you hadn't already guessed) and I can honestly say that the contents of this unattended table has lately become one of my chief sources of interest and entertainment.

The table is low, rickety, lopsided. The green oilcloth cover is faded by the sun. Invariably dotted about on it are little heaps of wilting garden produce. There might be four knobbly potatoes. Or three thin leeks held together with an elastic band. Or one tomato. Sometimes a small lettuce. Occasionally a posy of flowers. You put your coins in a marmalade jar.

The produce for sale here looks poor stuff compared with the prodigious decontaminated uniformities one sees in the supermarket vegetable aisle. I felt sorry for it at first, and sorry, too, for whoever was trying to sell it. Yet those first leeks I took home — limp, undersized things at three for 50 pence — were the most delicious and leekiest tasting leeks I'd tasted in years. As for the spuds, well, I'd almost forgotten what real ones tasted like until I carried four knobbly earth-encrusted ones home wrapped in newspaper and had them for tea.

The other remarkable thing about this honesty stall, apart from the disparity between the produce's lacklustre appearance and wonderful taste, is that there is always a thought for the day, handwritten on a page ripped from an old diary, and prevented by a smooth beach pebble from blowing away. Food for the mind, presumably, to complement that for the body. For a deserted table set outside a silent cottage in a deep country lane, these thoughts for the day seem slightly mad, even sinister.

I've had: 'The joys of evil flow away like a torrent.' And: 'A single word often betrays a great design.' Also: 'All is quiet, the army, the wind, and Neptune.'

These thoughts or warnings or quotations lead me to speculate on the nature and personality of the gardener. They suggested to my susceptible imagination that the gardener was perhaps a healer or a wise woman, or at the very least a cryptic old cottager steeped in folklore and superstition. Those thin leeks, for example, had of course been set when the moon was waning; the potatoes sown at the first sighting of a yellow wagtail in spring and on a rising tide; the visiting bees honoured as holy and told everything. But on every one of my visits to the table the old cottage was silent, and never a soul about, not even a dog or a cat or a hesitant hen, and never any money in the jar to indicate other transactions. But eternally there was the undersized, unenticing produce; always the new thought for the day handwritten on the torn diary page.

And then at last I came sweating around the bend in the lane one day, and when in sight of the table and the cottage I heard voices: raised, angry voices. I felt in my jeans for my coins and went to the table. While I studied my choice of vegetables, two men of late middle age faced one another in the garden, furious with one another. Their desire to represent their feelings to one another seemed to run deeper than the feelings themselves. I think they were in love.

'Graham. We. Are. Finished,' said one, finally. He made a petulant little mime with thumb and forefinger of an irrevocable fastening of a short invisible zip that floated in the air between their faces. Then he turned and stalked away. I dropped 20 pence in the jar, picked up an onion and cocked my head to read the thought for the day. It was a question. It said: 'Is faith without action a sincere faith?'

AN ABJECT COWARD
29 June 2013

Alone and lonely, I once met a woman in a train on the Mombasa to Nairobi 'Lunatic Express' line. She was seated opposite me in the compartment, next to her husband. The three of us had the compartment to ourselves. It was early in the morning. I've forgotten what the sleeping arrangements had been the night before. I think perhaps the husband and I had bedded down together and she'd rejoined him in the morning. Her husband had then left the compartment to go to the lavatory or dining car, and she and I had begun to talk.

She'd met and married the husband after a whirlwind romance a year before, she told me, and they'd opened and run a small restaurant together up the coast at Lamu. All very idyllic and romantic, perhaps, but the business had failed, then the marriage. They had sold up and were returning to Nairobi where they had agreed to part for three months to think things over independently. She intended honouring that agreement by trying to re-imagine a future with her husband, she said, but she already knew that it was no longer what she wanted. Through the window, brilliantly lit by early morning sunlight, was heavenly acacia savannah populated with zebra and Grant's and Thomson's gazelle.

Then I told her about myself and my recent past, a relatively uninteresting tale, and then the train came off the rails. I don't suppose we were going very fast because neither of us noticed the derailment at the time, so engrossed were we in each other's life stories. All I can remember of it is looking out of the window and suddenly realising that we were stationary and hadn't moved for a long while. Then her husband returned and told us the train was badly derailed, then he went off again to find out more, and his wife and I resumed our exchange of confidences.

She and I talked for the rest of the morning and into the afternoon, unconscious of time passing, while outside the window zebra and gazelle cropped the grass. The husband reappeared and disappeared at intervals. He thought that in all probability we would be stranded there for a couple of days. He was a pleasant, intelligent, polite man and I liked him. And I liked his wife, too, very much. I can't tell you what she looked like. I don't think her appearance registered with me much because it was immaterial. My strongest impressions were intuitive ones of a delightful, sympathetic personality. We were two sides of the same coin. At one point we stopped talking and examined one another's faces with curiosity and surprise at the strength of our improbable affinity, at which we both suddenly laughed, and then we laughed again at the way our laughter had mirrored one other.

Then a white man put his head through the compartment door and said he had managed to get a message through to Nairobi and a car sent out. There was space in this car for one more paying passenger. The car had arrived and they were leaving right away. He spoke with the brisk neutrality of a businessman. 'I'll come with you,' I said. 'Fine. Bring your luggage down to the dining car,' he said. Then he was gone.

I can only suppose I must have panicked. I stood up and hauled my rucksack off the luggage rack and quickly got my bits and pieces together. Following our warm and easy intimacy, my haste to get going was unseemly, indecent. But I must have fully realised that something momentous had occurred between us, because at the very last moment before leaving her I remembered something. In my trouser pocket was a polished brown nut that an alcoholic, sun-bleached old beachcomber had given to me a few days earlier in exchange for a bottle of Castle. He'd told me with utmost seriousness that this type of nut was esteemed locally as having certain magical properties. Keep it with you and it will attract a kindred spirit to you, he said. Perhaps even a wife. If it happened, I would recognise it immediately, he said. I should then place the love nut in that person's palm as a sign of recognition and a gift of welcome.

I asked her to hold out her hand. She opened her palm between us and I placed the nut in the centre and told her what it was and what was its significance. She closed her fingers and looked away from me and out of the window. And that last image of her is the one that I've retained in my mind ever since: of her looking distractedly out of the window of the derailed train, her arm still extended, and her fingers lightly closed over my gift of welcome.

BILDERBERG
13 July 2013

Searching the web for information about the enigmatic
Bilderberg group, I came across a website called Who
Controls America? It's a simple site to navigate: you click
on 'White House' or 'Wall Street' or 'Hollywood' and
you get a list of the main players and a big colour photo
of each from the neck up. (You know where I'm going
already, don't you?) Each face is identified as belonging to
a particular race or, if you prefer, heritage. At the bottom
of each list is a tally of the percentage of Jewish people
on that list, the percentage of Jewish people in the US
population at large (2 per cent, it says), and the factor by
which Jews are therefore overrepresented. On the White
House list, for example, 9 out of 11 of the 'current or
former senior advisers' to President Obama are identified
as Jewish. The implication being, presumably, that this
overrepresentation of this minority is evidence of a world
conspiracy to shaft the goyim. Leaving that aside, however,
and assuming the list doesn't disingenuously include
cleaners and tea ladies, I still found the preponderance a
little surprising.

Apart from the lineage of bullocks, we don't know
anything here in Devon. We don't even pretend to know
anything. So I carried my small surprise up to London
last week, to this year's very wonderful *Spectator* Summer
'At Home' party. And at the start, while I was still sober,
I brought the question up in the first conversation I had,

which happened to be with Mr Con Coughlin, executive foreign editor of the *Daily Telegraph*.

I approached the question much as I have here, by first describing the Who Controls America? website. But Con Coughlin saw where I was coming from a country mile away. Long before I'd arrived, he was smiling sadly yet lovingly at me, and shaking his head, as though I were a close brother with a sad history of schizophrenia, who, after a long and blessed period of wellness, had suddenly started complaining again that his television was bugged by the CIA.

And then a momentary darkening of the sky made us both look up at the appearance of the kindly figure of Spectator's drinks correspondent, Mr Bruce Anderson. I have often noticed and admired how the heavyweight London journalists refuse to bother with such bourgeois niceties as greetings, handshakes or indeed preliminaries of any kind. They treat one another as ubiquities. A new arrival not seen for weeks or months is accepted complacently, as if they are reappearing after leaving the room for a minute or two.

'Jeremy was just asking whether the Jews ran the world,' said Con, as Bruce 'the Beast' Anderson hove to, puffing slightly. 'Oh, I wish they would!' he said, entering in seamlessly, as though he'd been handed the question on a folded piece of paper five hours before. Satisfied by these candid reactions — and slightly disappointed that humanity is apparently more anaemic than I had hoped or imagined — I got drunk.

The party was tremendous, like going to heaven. Everyone in our part of the garden was so singular and friendly, and every conversation so witty or somehow engaging, emigration to other parts wasn't straightforward, and I relapsed into parochialism. Our bower had its own little bar, which I had patronised also last year, that is until I passed out under a nearby bush. It was the same barman. He greeted me with something approaching love and thereafter took it as both a personal and professional failure if he spotted that my tall drink — Gawd knows what he put in it — was ever less than spilling out all over the place.

And it was here (to my profoundest regret afterwards) that I broke my promise to myself not to bore anyone with my news. Coming up on the train I'd had a strong word with myself not to mention it at all costs. Vain hope. Sober I can be a model of modesty, propriety and restraint. Drunk: not so much. All too predictably there came a point in the evening when someone said, 'How are you?' and I replied, 'I've got fucking cancer.' I have. Prostate and spreading. Two, maybe three lymph nodes. They are going to try to zap it. It might be possible to keep it at bay for a few years yet, they say. But please. *The Spectator* Summer party?

And now that all sense of decorum had deserted me, I started telling everyone — friends, strangers, even the barman. First I told it bitterly, then boastfully, then hilariously. Come the end I was using it as a chat-up line. And though horribly ashamed the next day, I also felt somehow differently about my carcinoma, and inexplicably better for having told it. But it was the wrong place. And so is this! I shan't mention it here again. I promise.

PERIOD DRAMA
20 July 2013

We were watching *Top Gear*. I was sitting on a wobbly fold-up chair at a rickety garden table in a newly decorated, though otherwise empty first-floor flat. The garden furniture was there because the estate agent said it was better to have something in the sitting room rather than nothing at all, otherwise the place might have a desolate, depressing air that might put the viewers off. My boy has borrowed the flat from a friend for a couple of days while he considers his options. He, poor lad, was sitting at the table also, feeling the heat and desolate with grief. But he was maintaining his dignity. On the table was a flimsy floral tablecloth, and on that a copy of the *Sun* newspaper.

'She'll come round in a minute and you'll look back on this and laugh,' I said. He focused his brown eyes sceptically on mine for a moment then returned them to the irrepressible Jeremy Clarkson. He and his fellow petrolheads, and the adoring audience, which was massed and grinning around him, didn't appear to have a care in the world, nor did they seem to have the capacity to have a care in the world. There was a very beautiful, sexy, beaming woman in the front row, as there usually is, and I suddenly desired to be her, or to be united with her, with a violent desperation that surprised and appalled me.

The heat in the flat was stifling. Every window in the flat was flung wide open to invite a breeze — though none came. The three musketeers were in Spain racing supercars around the empty streets of a half-finished housing project and mucking about in a deserted brand-new airport. But my thoughts kept straying.

I looked down at my narrow, unfamiliar, sandalled feet and studied the broken nail on my big toe. Then I studied my knobbly knees, one crossed over another, and let my eyes wander over the grass stains on my black Adidas shorts. I'd put them on the wrong way round again, I noticed. Misled by the position of the side pockets, I put them on back to front probably nine times out of ten.

The flat was the only private property on a purpose-built estate for servicemen and women. Servicemen were strolling back and forth on the tarmac below with their shirts off. Someone was having a barbeque. Smoke curling from an end-block garden told where. A man with the toned body of a fitness fanatic, and a can of Red Stripe dangling from his fingertips, walked slowly around my car — an old Mercedes pillarless coupé — admiring it, I think. There aren't many of these left in Britain now. The front is a bit boxy, but viewed from the side the car is as aesthetically pleasing as a Turner. A security patrol van cruised by at less than a walking pace. The driver's arm was hanging out of the window. The arm raised itself a few inches to acknowledge the car enthusiast and fell back again.

'I'm not having it,' I said. 'And neither should you be!'

My boy regarded me calmly and candidly for a moment. The look was meant to suggest that of the two of us at the table it was I who needed to adjust my understanding to the present reality, and not him. 'I know her. It's over,' he said. Then he took his mother's big brown tragicomic eyes back to the television screen.

Whatever else is happening in my life, I'm having a love affair with one of his children. (The other is contentedly absorbed by his inner world and shows few signs so far of wanting to transfer to the outer, even at two.) From a purely selfish perspective, my future happiness was as threatened as my boy's. Perhaps more so. And this was the exact moment I realised that this was the reality, and that my world had changed. Up to this point I had lightly dismissed the recent split as temporary; a hackneyed scene from a popular, much repeated period drama, in which I've played a sagacious and kindly old nincompoop with his wig awry. Now I was frightened. 'Well, I'm not having it,' I said.

It sounded hollow. My boy stood and went into the kitchen to look for something to use as an ashtray. I could see him through the hatch rummaging through a wall cupboard. Then he returned to the table with the glass lid of an ovenproof dish and placed it between us. I felt the stirrings of a breeze enter the room and fan my cheek on its way past. My boy reached for his pouch of smuggled tobacco. The *Top Gear* audience roared with sycophantic laughter. Outside, a dove called mellifluously.

BEAUTIFUL POLICE
27 July 2013

How was your journey?' I said. In summer, the place next door is let to visitors on a weekly basis. We share a driveway, and I generally get to meet whoever comes to stay. Last week's visitors were German. The father and the two teenage boys were tall, gangling and mild. I met them soon after they had arrived and were unpacking the car. Silent, gnomic presences in the background, the sons continued dutifully with the unloading, leaving it to their parents to interact with the inquisitive natives.

They'd driven from Germany, said the Dad. Motoring across Belgium and France was easy. From Dover to Devon was less so. It was an ordeal, frankly. Not the least of their trouble was that somebody had chosen to commit suicide by throwing themselves from a motorway bridge and they'd been stuck in the resulting jam for hours.

A few days later I encountered them again in the driveway as they unpacked the car after a day on the beach. They seemed dazed, perhaps by the blistering heat. 'How are you getting on?' I said. The narrowness of the country lanes was testing his courage, admitted the Dad. The beaches were very nice, though, interpolated the Mum, and the scenery was oh so nice. 'But the people are a little crazy, no?'

She explained that last evening the family was enjoying a quiet meal in a pub when a mass brawl had erupted at the bar. 'We thought the pub looked so nice, so quiet, and we were eating our fish and chips and suddenly everybody was fighting and throwing chairs,' she said. Then the police came. The situation after that she described as 'very police'. The policewoman who took a statement from them was 'so nice, so beautiful'.

I encountered the family again early next morning. They were sitting in their car about to set off somewhere. Dad looked relieved to see me. He hopped out of the car to pick my brains. They were going on Dartmoor for the day, he said. Could I please give him directions avoiding the narrowest roads if possible, and recommend a nice place to head for? I most certainly could, I said, for little did he know that I am a mad evangelist for the place.

I ran indoors for my Ordinance Survey Outdoor Leisure map 28 held together with orange duct tape. I spread out the map on the bonnet of his car, put my fingernail under Haytor, and suggested he went there. It's a Mecca for day trippers, I said, apologetically. But the road to Haytor is the widest and the least tortuous approach; the views from Haytor the most spectacular in Devon; and there is a car park, tourist information office and gift shop. He might not want to hang around there, I said, but he could get his bearings from the granite outcrop if he decided to hike off into the stony wilderness behind it. And if the mood took him, he could buy a souvenir genuine hide keyring from the gift shop afterwards.

As their car drew up later that evening, I went out to greet them. 'How was Dartmoor?' I said, failing to keep the proprietorial tone out of my voice. Their lanky sons were their usual silent, enigmatic selves; mother and father looked stricken, however.

They had gone to Haytor, as I'd suggested, said Dad. They'd walked up the hill then climbed to about halfway up the 100-foot high tor when they'd heard shouting. At the summit, they learnt from other tourists that a young woman and a small boy had just fallen to their deaths. (Later, on the car radio, they'd learnt that the woman had set the boy on her shoulders and jumped deliberately.) The emergency services, including a police helicopter, were quickly on the scene and Mum was interviewed by our beautiful police again.

But from this desperately tragic event, the mother had selected, seemingly at random, a particular aspect on which to vent her perhaps confused emotions. What had most impressed and outraged her sensibilities, she claimed, was the awful behaviour of the public. From the sudden increase in traffic, it was obvious to her that once news of the tragedy had spread, ghouls had jumped in their cars and made purposefully for the beauty spot. Elderly couples in collapsible chairs, their mouths crammed with food, she said, were watching the recovery of the bodies avidly through binoculars, as though at a sporting event. Never before had she seen such crass behaviour as she had witnessed that afternoon. She didn't know whether to laugh or cry, she said, verging now on the latter.

'We English are a crass and brutal nation,' I said, by way of a tongue-in-cheek explanation, 'because they don't bother educating us. But we have our good points.'

'I hope so,' she said with passionate sincerity, tears springing into her eyes. 'I really hope so.'

BILLY
23 August 2013

In 1984 I was 27. Since leaving school I had done unskilled manual labour, when I could get any. Then I worked as a nursing assistant and then a trainee nurse in an 840-bed psychiatric hospital at Goodmayes in Essex, formerly the West Ham Lunatic Asylum. It was like a walled town. I ate, slept and socialised in there and became institutionalised and a bit mad, I believe.

In ordinary life, among relatively sane people, one becomes fairly confident about the parameters of so-called normal human behaviour. They are narrow parameters, and all the time getting narrower, I think. But if you live in a large mental hospital, these parameters widen drastically, or even disappear altogether. And after a time one comes to relish and prefer the greater variety of human behaviour, and the daily surprises occurring within the crenelated walls, and life outside becomes insipid. I was sacked finally, for, among other things, 'throwing human excrement at members of the public'.

After that I led an itinerant existence performing more unskilled labour. I mucked out pigs. I cleared builders' rubble on piece-work. Around this time, too, I had a silly season, and became familiar with the protocol of the magistrates' court. I was up before the garden gate about once a week, and I was glad of the unusually close attention that was paid to my life by the well-meaning people who work in them.

I've been thinking about this period of my life a lot lately, after reading in the newspapers about the 'allegation of a sexual nature' that has recently been made to the South Yorkshire police about Cliff Richard. It was said to have taken place at a Billy Graham Christian faith rally at Sheffield United's Bramall Lane football ground in 1985. Apparently, there were 47,000 people packed into the stadium that night, and a total of 200,000 people came to hear him speak over five nights — a surprisingly large number. And reading about that reminded me that Billy Graham also toured Britain's football stadiums in 1984, one of which was Ashton Gate, home of Bristol City. For I was there on one of the four successive nights he spoke, and the stadium was packed then, too. Thirty thousand spectators, a 2,000-strong choir, the singer George Hamilton IV as a warm-up, and then the world famous evangelist Billy Graham got up to speak.

He spoke softly but mesmerically. 'Remember the tape at Watergate?' he said, looking around the stadium. 'They had everything recorded in the rooms in the White House. They had it on tape. When you stand at the judgment of God he will say to the Angels: "Let's listen to the tapes!"'

I could well imagine it. I could imagine standing there at the gates, the angels and I gathered around one of those old-fashioned tape recorders, and a manicured angelic forefinger being extended and pressing 'play'. And I imagined that everybody listening would very quickly have heard all they needed to hear. At that time I had broken about six of the Ten Commandments. I was dwelling in the tents of wickedness.

'The wages of sin is death,' said Billy Graham. 'Hell begins here, but hell is to come as well. You won't find the answers in drugs or sex. Change your heart, your way of living.'

I knew it already. The man was quite right. I'd been taught about sin since I was small. I knew about rotten wages. I knew about drugs, not that I could ever afford many. I didn't know much about sex, but I was perfectly willing to lump it in with drugs and hell on Billy Graham's say-so. He was a powerful speaker. You listened to him. And then came the moment that many of us had been eagerly awaiting. The trademark of a Billy Graham rally was the call to faith; the invitation to come to the front in a public declaration of repentance. And here it came.

'So now I am going to ask you to get up out of your seat and say, by coming up here, that you are going to open your heart to Christ. You must get up and walk. It may take two or three minutes and you will receive a prayer and some literature.'

I didn't walk. I was so desperate for a reboot, I climbed over the wall and I sprinted on to that pitch, one of the first to arrive in the centre circle. There were many other sprinters. For those like us, Billy Graham might as well have mounted the lectern, cut out the chat, raised a starting pistol above his head, and fired it. More than 2,000 souls ran, walked or sauntered on to the pitch that night and gave their hearts to Jesus. I wonder how they're all doing.

TREV PULLS
3 September 2013

I haven't been out for three weeks and I'm up for a big night. To prove it I'm wearing my cowboy shirt with silver buttons and crimson roses embroidered on the shoulders. I ring Trev to check in and say I'm just leaving the house. So that we don't have to worry about last orders, I tell him, I've got two tickets for a reggae disco at a bar with a late licence. 'It's been a long time, bud!' he says.

'How's the old love life?' I say. 'Are you still seeing that Juliet?' Trev's love life conforms to the rules of a narrow, traditional genre, but within these constraints it is endlessly entertaining. He is 55 or something. Juliet is 18. She and her Mum live around the corner from Trev and she pops in to see him from time to time.

I was there when they first met. Her Mum had invited a few noted local pissheads back to the house after the pub, including Trevor and myself. Juliet was there, already head-lollingly drunk and Trev exposed himself to her, I remember, by way of a witty introduction. The next day they were driving around in his old Range Rover with her head in his lap, and he rang to tell me. Then he put her on the phone. 'A'right dude?' she drawled. 'Yes, thank you,' I said. For all I know, Juliet has the mental range and stature of a Simone de Beauvoir and is seeking transcendence. But it was impossible to tell, and justly credit her for it, because her vocabulary was so small. The list of marine animals — both higher and lower —

found to have a larger vocabulary than Juliet's is growing longer every year.

The first time she stayed the night, Trev told me, there came a violent hammering on his front door at about three in the morning. Trev put on his dressing-gown and went to see who it was. It was Juliet's Mum. She was standing there with her current boyfriend, a leading ne'er do well. They'd not come, as Trev thought, to rescue her daughter and give him a mouthful. Far from it. They said they were sorry to disturb him but they'd seen his light still on, and did he by any chance have the phone number of the all-night cheap booze home delivery service that everyone was talking about?

'Juliet?' said Trev. 'Well, she still comes round to shag me now and again, if that's what you mean, but to be honest she's a pain in the ass and I try to discourage her. Poor little maid,' he added, always the man for seeing, if not the whole, then certainly the wider picture.

I arrange to meet Trev in our usual pub about nine o'clock. I have a few anaesthetising scoops in another, quieter pub before wandering along for the fray at quarter past. The pub is packed out, and absolutely 'bangin" as Juliet might say. I'm wordlessly offered a toke on a collapsed single skinner on the way in. Inside, a live covers band is getting into its raucous stride and everyone seems to have already achieved that separation from reality that is the entire point of going out. There must be ecstasy or MDMA in circulation this evening, too; I can feel the love. An insanely loved-up woman I barely know hugs me and hangs from my neck, bleating my name. At the same time, this bloke whose psychosis is pretty much permanent, and who is always cadging drinks off me, cups his mouth to my ear and whispers urgently, 'Just one. Please. I'm begging you, man. Just one.'

The barmaid sets a pint before me without my asking. 'And one for Teddy here,' I say. And Ted, overcome with gratitude and brotherly love, secretly reveals something down around his groin area, as though he's allowing me a glimpse of a pocket revolver, except it's a whacking great lump of hashish, black, an ounce at least. And he breaks off a madly generous lump and puts it in my hand.

Reaching up and placing my pint on a shelf above the door, I go outside among the smokers again. Trev's out here, just arrived. As he steps forward to greet me with a hug, a young woman with blonde pigtails glides between us. Trev does his comedy sex-maniac face then reaches out and yanks her back by a pigtail. And that's it. Game over. She's his for the night, apparently. He's pulled -- in the most literal sense possible -- and I've lost my drinking partner before we've even bloody well started. Even Trev can't believe it. He's apologetic. 'Sorry, bud,' he says. 'Open your mouth and shut your eyes,' I say forgivingly, reaching for the lump Ted gave me.

KEEP CALM!
7 September 2013

We picked up the key to the caravan, let ourselves in, ascertained the phone signal situation (none) and went to the beach. Polzeath beach is the kind of bucket-and-spade beach Janet and John's Mummy and Daddy might have chosen for their annual holiday. First, soft white sand ideal for burying Mummy; then a broad shining plain of hard, smooth sand, ideal for sandcastles, dam projects, or tunnelling to Australia; then gentle inch-deep wavelets — spent rollers — for toddlers and oldies to paddle in. Then flags. Then thundering surf crowded with Neoprene figures, all shapes, sizes and ages, some of them screaming, and riderless surfboards flipped skywards; each successive wave a chaotic and exhilarating drama.

We were an all-male, three-generation line-up this year: me, my boy and my boy's two young sons. At the entrance to the beach all save my boy took off our socks and shoes and stuffed them into our bucket. Four abreast and squinting into the brightness, we progressed pale-footed across soft then hard sand towards the line of surf. My boy was depressed and preoccupied. His younger son was hanging on to his hand, grizzling. His elder son, however, was prancing ahead, shrieking ecstatic gibberish, and dancing dementedly in every rock pool. I saw only one item of litter: a Moët and Chandon champagne cork.

We possessed neither wetsuits nor boards, but we were equipped with the aforementioned bucket, blue, and a bright red spade. So we scouted some low, mussel-coated rocks, found a suitable cockpit-sized declivity, and grandad excavated thick, enclosing ramparts, so that when the tide came up, we could stand behind them and calmly defy the sea, until finally it breached and overcame them, whereupon grandad would do his startling impression of a German U-boat klaxon signalling action stations, and we would scramble to safety over the rocks.

While I laboured, my boy sat on a rock, rolled a fag, checked his phone again, found to his surprise that he had one bar, immediately made a call, and had an increasingly sharp altercation with his ex-partner for ten minutes, while his younger son clung to his trouser legs and cried. A smooth-faced young lad tripping over the rocks saw my effort, stopped, and said, 'That's what I call not bad, actually.' I topped off the ramparts with a castellation of mud pies and we took up our positions within.

A calm, the first of our holiday, descended upon us. United behind our enclosing wall, we silently contemplated the encroaching waves, each of us closed off and occupied with our own private thoughts and fantasies. The lip of an advanced wave tipped into the moat, filling it, and withdrew. At the same time an elderly man, all head and earlobes, tropical tan, effete calves sticking out of the bottom of his wetsuit, and that invisible patina of class and authority, making an orderly retreat from the incoming tide, stopped, impressed perhaps by our Buddha-like impassivity as much as by my ramparts.

'My word!' he announced. 'Magnificent! Will you be bringing up guns?' They were on the way, I told him, not smiling. 'What kind?' he said. Howitzers, I said. He pouted in professional disapproval. 'Too slow. Mind if I stick around as an observer?' My boy rolled his eyes at me. His small sons eyed the man with profound suspicion. He took up a strategic position nearby, seating himself comfortably on a smooth rock.

A wave in the van of the rapidly advancing tide glided to the foot of our ramparts, filled the moat again and withdrew. I gave a loud burst on the U-boat klaxon. The elder boy shrieked for joy; the younger burst into tears. The big-ear-lobed man — I had him down as a retired sea lord or something — made a fist and spoke calmly into it, as into the mouthpiece of a ship's broadcasting system.

'Remain calm. Work together. Remember your training. Steel your hearts. Honour your nation. You have been superbly trained, and for eventualities such as this. Nothing will occur for which we are unprepared. And at the first opportunity we will hit back, I can promise you, and with everything that we have. When we've finished with them, the buggers won't know what hit them.'

I looked askance at this old man. His fist still to his mouth, he flashed me a happy warrior look with his eyes. The third wave undermined our redoubt, the fourth breached it, the fifth and sixth overwhelmed it, and we abandoned our precarious position, piggy-backing the children over the rocks. 'Keep calm!' counselled the authoritative voice through the curled fist. 'Remember your training! Do your duty!'

Anybody who thinks our Prime Minister's was slumming it by choosing Polzeath for his annual holiday couldn't be more wrong. There he was in fact entirely surrounded by his own powerful social class, phone signal or no phone signal.

QUIZ NIGHT
14 September 2013

One evening last week, I trotted over to the caravan site's clubhouse to use the wifi and pick up emails. One email was from a friend who reported that someone had described me, after meeting me for the first time, as an 'intellectual'. Unsure whether to be flattered or appalled by this misjudgment, I ordered a hot panini (cheese and red onion) to save cooking dinner back at the caravan and running the battery down on the smoke detector, which was going off so often when I cooked that I'd begun using it as a timer.

As I rammed the panini into my face, an elderly man, with what was almost certainly a chapel Christian face, came and set up a table, chair and microphone in a central position. Another smaller, facetious-looking fellow came round issuing biros, clipboards and paper. 'You'll join us for the quiz,' he said. My cheeks bulging with panini, I shook my head. He gave me a clipboard and biro anyway.

He then ordered me to move across and join a team consisting of a woman and her daughter who'd brought three hens on holiday with them. I'd noticed them — three plump brown hens in a wood and wire coop — on my daily jog around the site. Once I'd stopped near the coop for a breather, and the woman had come out and presented me with a freshly collected egg, which I'd jogged back with, smooth and still warm in my hand. She and her daughter were drinking Harvey Wallbangers.

Then the facetious-looking man decided instead that I should join forces with a late arrival, who drew up a chair opposite mine. He was also drinking Harvey Wallbangers. (I assumed this was due to a special promotion rather than to a peculiarity of the local Cornish culture.) He tipped back his head and downed his first as though it were nothing stronger than freshly squeezed orange juice, then called immediately for another. When that came, he raised it to his lips, threw back his head again, but managed to restrain himself and only allow half of it to tip down his throat. He was about 65 years old. He had humorous eyes and a sharp, youthful haircut. His voice was low and deeply Cornish. The quizmaster for Jesus blew on the mike, called for quiet and began to read from his prepared list of questions. I took up the biro.

My team mate was a sportsman and a team player. He was anxious to win and give his all for the cause. At the asking of each question, he went into paroxysms of agony and despair. He invariably knew the answer. It was just a question of ransacking his brains until he lighted on it. The head slumped forward until his chin was resting on his chest, as though he were deep in prayer. The squeezed shut eyelids pressed the eyeballs back into his head, perhaps to exert extra pressure on the brain. But the answer was most often tantalisingly just out of reach. And then he would lift his head and blink in surprise, as though he'd just regained consciousness, shake his head in sorrow and profound regret, and I would write down the correct answer. For the majority of the questions, though carefully thought-out, were surprisingly easy. What is the national bird of the United States? What is the other name of the 'killer whale'? And so on.

But as luck would have it, fortified by several additional, urgently called-for Harvey Wallbangers, my partner dug deep and found the answers to those questions I couldn't answer. The number of years celebrated by a coral wedding anniversary. The number of books of the Old Testament. And best of all, the name of Steptoe and Son's horse (Hercules). This last answer was dredged up from the depths after a titanic mental struggle, during which his chin rested on his chest for so long that I assumed he had fallen asleep.

To the great surprise of both of us, we won the quiz by a country mile. We rose to a patter of reluctant, jealous applause and stepped forward to collect our boxes of chocolates. Before accepting his, however, my team mate's conscience got the better of him and he took up the microphone. He had a confession to make, he said. He had also taken part in last week's quiz, and this week's questions were exactly the same as last week's. But he wanted to assure everybody that during the week the answers had all completely gone from his mind except Steptoe's horse. And as we had won the quiz by so many points, he said, he had no other qualms about accepting the prize. 'Excuse me, are you a teacher or something?' said a lad on one of the other teams as I made my way back to my seat.

CICADAS
24 September 2013

Golly my testicles are shrinking fast. At this rate by Christmas they'll be down to the size of garden peas. And I might have breasts on the way, too, it says on page 92 of the hormone injection contraindications leaflet. Fantastic! Just what I've always wanted.

After two days at the seaside at St Raphaël, me and my incredible shrinking knackers headed inland to a busy, famously pretty little village in the hills. Friends — a sculptor and his wife — put me up in their tall rented house on the plane tree-shaded square for five days. I arrived in the middle of a local's all-day birthday party at which the 60-year-old, nut-brown hostess, wearing a tiny white bikini, was dancing on the tables, and my pale sculptor friend, magnificent in a thick Harris tweed kilt and enormous sporran, suffered a touch of sunstroke. This was my introduction to the local rosé, the fuller-bodied highly addictive sort, which became a blessed staple.

For four days the itinerary was roughly as follows. In the mornings, I walked in the stony hills, deafened at first by the cacophonous crepitations of the cicadas. But I quickly grew accustomed to the extraordinary noise then was largely unconscious of it. But sometimes, when an idle thought triggered a heightened emotion, this strange, other-worldly sound (something like the crackling of overhead high-voltage electricity) would re-enter my consciousness with a dramatically increased intensity.

Then as the emotion gradually subsided, the crepitations would fade away also. It was as though the small dramas of a consciousness even as unexciting as mine were being carefully monitored and imitated by an audience of hundreds of thousands of sympathetic insects hidden in the trees.

It was the first week of August, and yet I rarely saw another soul. And from the eminences you could see for miles and miles across what looked like forested wilderness with not a road or a habitation or a pylon to spoil the view or to remind you of your place in the 21st century. Surprisingly big country, France.

In the afternoons I sat for my portrait. My sculptor friend also paints. I sat shirtless in a chair beside an open window. He crouched on his collapsible stool at an easel maybe six feet away. His canvas was about 15in. by 10in. and positioned at the same height as my head. He told me to look away and slightly up, and for a focusing point I made use of a painting on the wall of the kind of sun-baked village that one might see in a spaghetti western. It was a terrible painting but every afternoon I took a long walk through its alleys, and visited the whitewashed chapel to sit in the coolness and sometimes pray, and so I came to know the painting as a real place in my imagination, so whether the painting was any good or not finally was irrelevant.

After getting quickly over my initial self-consciousness at being intently scrutinised by a man who has been trained how to look and see, I found it a pleasant, relaxing experience to be painted. The window at my back gave out on to the aforementioned classically Provençal village square cooled by the shade of its plane trees and a trickling fountain. The square was decked out with café tables under jolly sunshades and tightly stretched awnings, at which trade was brisk from mid-morning till midnight.

Each afternoon, then, after a rosé-lubricated lunch, I sat in the cool dimness of that first-floor living room, next to the open window, chin tilted at the painting on the opposite wall, listening to the gentle hubbub wafting upwards from the busy square below. Punctuating the low hum of Gallic chatter might be the ring of one wafer-thin glass against another, an outpouring clatter of cutlery, the rude clank of a plate, the beserker squeals of infants playing beside the fountain, the unconscionable din of a passing motorbike, the yap yap of a small dog, the slightly anxious cooing of a dove, an electric guitar muted by distance, a raised voice, a tumble of laughter. And one afternoon, there came a clap of thunder out of an apparently blue sky that set the cicadas off like mad. And when the portrait was completed, I walked around and looked at it and saw for the first time what I looked like, which is quite something.

And in the evenings? Well, a couple of pints of lager, known there as formidables, and dinner under the umbrellas with bucketfuls of rosé, dancing, cognac with sugar cubes, and in my case the (to me) miraculous continuance of a delightful romance begun on the second evening with the stunning, raven-haired Ester from Hollywood, to whom I explained very early doors about my incredible shrinking testicles, but that, as they say, is another story.

MEET SUZY COMPETITION
12 October 2013

A surprisingly convivial atmosphere prevailed in the second-class carriage of the fast London-bound train when I stepped aboard at Bodmin. A loud, cheerful, messy young family was eating and drinking unrestrainedly, though it was not yet 11 o'clock. Cans of bitter and lager, not all of them unopened, were arrayed on several other tables. Animated conversation and uninhibited laughter were widespread. And — was it my imagination? — a Cornish national spirit presided, vivid with pleasure at the prospect of exchanging a green wet peninsular for the solidity of the metropolis.

As I moved down the carriage aisle searching for an empty seat, Cornish eyes lifted to meet mine, not shyly or slyly, but with friendly curiosity. Some to ascertain how quick on the uptake I was that this was the noisy party carriage; others to gauge what kind of a personality I was bringing to the affair.

I found a vacant seat beside a young woman in her late twenties wearing kneed, agricultural-looking jeans. As I sat, she greeted me cordially through protruding teeth. Her greeting was so unaffectedly welcoming, I wondered if we'd met before. In her hands was an unfranked letter, the address in capitals. She intercepted my glance and began to talk about it.

She was a massive Suzi Quatro fan, she said. She was a life subscription fan club member and she had seen Suzi in concert countless times. She'd travelled as far as Berlin to see her play. But she had only met Suzi — who is a lovely, lovely person — twice so far. This letter, she said, was her entry in a prize draw organised by the fan club to meet Suzi Quatro and take afternoon tea with her at her house in Essex.

(Oddly enough, I was travelling up for a 'Meet the Readers' afternoon tea party at the Spectator office. I considered confessing this as a kind of coincidence, but when I rehearsed it in my head, it sounded so far-fetched, even to me, that I doubted whether she'd believe it, so I decided to keep it to myself.)

She lifted her arms in pious devotion to her idol, crossed fingers on both hands and shook them to agitate her luck. 'I just love her,' she said with simple passion. 'I love everything about her. To sit down to afternoon tea with Suzi would be heaven to me. After that I could die happy,' she said. And she breathed out a long sigh of ineffable sadness.

'How many other people do you think will enter the draw?' I said in all seriousness, for I have form and a little expertise in this area. I once had my entry picked out at random from an entry bag of 80,000 to win an XR3i cabriolet. She leaned in, her arm against mine, confidentially. I was on her wavelength. The competition, she said, was run by the fan club. So her guess was between 2,500 and 3,000 max. Suzi was going to pick the winning entry out of the bag herself. She always does. And now here's the thing, she said, lowering her voice. When Suzi Quatro picks an envelope at random out of a bag, she always delves down to about halfway and picks the first one that comes to hand. Always. She doesn't muck about.

She never roots around or churns the envelopes or shakes the bag. Never. She shoots in her hand — she's right-handed — it goes halfway down, then it comes out again with the winning card or envelope.

So her plan was this. (Again the confidential tone, from one competition expert to another.) She had been waiting until exactly halfway between the competition's opening and closing dates, and now she was going to post in her entry, hoping it would end up halfway down the bag. Rather than post her entry from Cornwall, and it taking anything up to a week to get there, throwing out her calculations, she was taking the letter up to London to post it, hoping for an overnight delivery from there to Suzi's home in Essex.

One couldn't help but admire such meticulous planning. I really wanted her to win. But I couldn't also help wondering whether she wouldn't have done better to think outside the box. Surely it would have saved a lot of trouble, and been far more exciting, to have gone to Suzi Quatro's house, knocked on the door, and declared her love to Suzi Quatro's face when she came to answer it.

What a nice woman, though! Already she'd told me the secret of her heart and enrolled me as a co-conspirator. I looked out of the window to see where we'd got to, half expecting to be looking down over the Tamar river. I was shocked to find that we hadn't yet pulled away from the platform at Bodmin. Friendly sorts, the Cornish.

INTERNATIONAL
YOGA STAR
19 October 2013

I'd booked a private one-to-one session with her for an hour on the afternoon of the day she flew in. I'd booked it casually, thoughtlessly, on a recommendation, a month in advance, unaware of her reputation. I'd dutifully filled in the form she sent me, circling problem areas on a drawn representation of my body, and mailed it back. It was only as the appointment drew near that I began to take heed, when overhearing talk at the yoga centre, of the excitement at the imminent arrival from across the pond of the great Linda Strong (as we'll call her). The impression was of a St Paul scheduled to visit Antioch for a few weeks to whip the faithful into shape.

The day, then the hour, of our private session came. I arrived at the yoga centre in a lather after driving like a maniac to get there on time and sprinting up the hill. I'd had a stressful day and was off my head. Following my one-to-one session with Linda, I planned to have a good drink at a ska band gig and I was wearing my Fred Perry polo shirt and sweater.

The door of the yoga centre opens on to the changing area. I went in and there she was, in person, flown in from America that afternoon, now taking payment from the gent with whom she'd been having the one-to-one session before mine. One glance was enough to verify her credentials. Seeing was believing. Here was an athlete at her peak, radiating health, strength, poise, power. Above all, power. In that small room she was an overwhelming presence, formidable in skintight pants, resting her weight on one bare, muscular foot while accepting a cheque from a client.

She'd asked the bloke for £110. As he went, closing the door respectfully behind him, I said, 'Is that how much you are going to charge me?' 'It is,' she said. 'Unless you can't afford it.' It seemed a lot and I swore horribly. (As I say, I was a bit off my head.) Then I said, madly, 'I don't know whether you are going to stick your finger up my arse or give me a massage, or both, or what, but I'm all yours.'

She came close, facing me squarely. Her eyes wandered dubiously over my Fred Perry clobber. Hadn't I brought anything more suitable to wear, she said? I hadn't, I said. She reached down to my thigh and took a pinch of my jeans to see if the fabric had any stretch. 'We can work with you in your jeans,' she said. I took off my sweater, shoes and socks, and emptied my jeans pockets on to the bench. She studied my medical form to remind herself of my case. 'You fractured your pelvis in 2009,' she said. 'Interesting. How?' 'In a car crash after a football match,' I said. 'I was completely drunk. I hit a bus head-on and wrote the car off. I woke up in hospital on a trolley with a policeman standing over me. I was on my back for six weeks afterwards.'

She gave my form further perusal. 'It says here you are a journalist,' she said. 'Are you a sports journalist?' Before I could answer, a sky-blue 50mg Viagra tablet, from among the effects I was transferring from my jeans pockets to the bench, slipped through my fingers and fell on to the floor. Exactly like a tiny blue rugby ball, it bounced erratically and unpredictably from one side of the room to the other, while the international yoga teacher and I, fascinated spectators, watched it go. 'Do you need to get that?' she said.

She asked me to lie on the floor, which I did, and she stood astride me. From below she looked tremendous. She asked me to raise my pelvis towards her. I did this. 'Relax your jaw,' she said. 'You are tensing your jaw. Have you ever noticed how you tense your jaw?' I had a think. 'Occasionally, yes,' I said. 'In the past. When I've taken drugs.' 'Which drugs?' she said. 'LSD,' I said. 'Ah,' she said. 'Coke,' I said. 'Amphetamine, MDMA, mushrooms.' 'Jeremy,' she said. She was a colossus with a serious face. 'The question I think that you have to ask yourself is a very simple one. It is this. Do you want to live or do you want to die? It's up to you to decide.'

It was indeed a great question. It was a question that was easily worth £110. If I'd turned up in a lather and she'd asked me that question without teaching me any of those exercises, and then sent me away again, it would have been worth it. I paid up without demur, determined to go away and think about it.

GASH WOOD
2 November 2013

We'd being trying to meet for lunch for weeks, but always something had got in the way and either she or I had had to cancel. But at long last we'd managed it, and after two pleasant hours we emerged from the fish restaurant and made our way along the sea front towards the car park, still marvelling at the achievement.

We hadn't gone far when she noticed two planks leaning against a wall. They were six by twos, each about 2ft long. The sight of these planks seemed to cause her to lose the ballerina's poise that she'd maintained throughout lunch. She became agitated and started hopping from foot to foot.

An absent person was putting in a new window frame. The job was half-finished. It was unclear whether the planks were gash, or materials essential to completion, or a loose, rather abstract embodiment of the concept of a safety barrier.

'Should I just take them, do you think?' she said, almost beside herself. 'They are exactly what I need.' I imagined she was thinking of doing a spot of do-it-yourself. Shelves, perhaps. I'm not above inexpensive improvisation of that kind myself. And a little light thieving on our first date would certainly have cemented whatever tentative connection we had already made across the luncheon table.

There were lots of people about and the planks were not without value. The sudden alteration in my behaviour from well-fed boulevardier to cautious spiv gave her a start and the moment was lost. A delightfully spontaneous post-prandial adventure was strangled at birth. 'I'd better ask first, hadn't I?' she said. She said it as if she were trotting out moral positions until she lighted on one I approved of. I was still doing my impression of Private Walker checking to see if the coast was clear.

The wall and window belonged to another busy restaurant. 'Let's ask,' she said. We pushed our way in through two glass doors and people with full stomachs coming out. The waitresses looked sweaty and harassed. Nevertheless one quickly came bustling over and mustered every remaining atom of politeness to put herself at our service. She was cockney. 'Hallo! You have some wood outside,' was how my lunch partner began to explain her plank love.

We'd met at the gym. Before today I'd only ever seen her at the gym. Before today I could hardly have conceived of her as a person who existed outside of a gym or wore anything but shorts and trainers. So while she gradually enlightened the initially puzzled waitress, I marvelled anew at the sight of this unfamiliar woman in jeans and street shoes. She is very petite, almost minute, and the waitress was tall and handsome, and she was looking up at the waitress as one might look up at the Shard. Before today, all of our conversations had been brief, snatched, gym conversations, with month-long gaps, often with one or other of us contorting ourselves on a warm-up mat. From these conversations I gathered that she is a hard-working and devoted Mum on the one hand, and a fanatical martial artist on the other. She holds black belts in karate, taekwondo and judo. Her karate club practises 'full-contact' karate sparring, she once told me. 'Don't you get injured?' I'd said, horrified. I used to get quite badly injured doing 'no-contact' karate, I said.

And the more she reluctantly revealed about herself, the more I realised that this tiny, smiling, modest, unfailingly courteous, superfit woman quietly followed the way of the warrior. After that I would bow to her on sight, and she'd laugh, but I meant it. It was her warrior courteousness that accounted for the brevity of our gym conversations; she imagined that I thought as she did; that to chatter in the gym was slovenly.

For lunch she'd had the soup of the day. She'd taken three quarters of an hour to eat that and a lump of plain bread, while exclaiming all the while what a wonderful treat she was having. She sat with her back straight and she inclined gracefully forward from the base of her spine to meet her soup spoon halfway. She laughingly confided that the cappuccino afterwards was a rare and thrilling indulgence.

By the end of their conversation about the wood, she and the tired waitress were as close as sisters. The waitress was sorry but she could only take down a phone number and pass it to the owner later in the day. As we walked back out of the restaurant together, I said, 'We should have just nicked them. What did you want them for, anyway?' She looked at me as though weighing me up to decide whether I was worth the telling. 'I'm a knife thrower,' she said with simple modesty. 'And they'd make perfect targets.'

JOINT
23 November 2013

The beer garden at the back of the pub was empty, save one woman sitting alone at a table contemplating a pint glass. It was Saturday night, early, already dark. I placed my carnival glass of Kirin Ichiban on the table next to hers and sat down. The beer garden was floodlit with blue and orange light. The stars were out.

I craned my head forward, sucked up an inch of cold lager without using my hands and looked sideways at the woman on the next table. I noticed a reaction to the mouthful of chilled beer on a cellular level. The woman looked miles away. 'If you're interested in a chat,' I said, 'this is the most sensible I'm going to be all night, so we should have it now.' She backed out of her reverie and regarded me. 'OK,' she said. 'What shall we talk about?'

'How's your love life?' I suggested. She rolled her eyes. 'Completely out of hand,' she said. 'Ridiculous. I wouldn't even know where to start.' But she had a stab at it, with approximate statistics, and then attempted a broad outline of a recent crisis, the result of which was her sitting outside on this chilly Saturday evening savouring a pint and some longed-for solitude.

Three chaps came out into the garden carrying full pints and joined her at her table without a trace of formality or a greeting. Regulars, presumably. The gang. Then another chap arrived, wearing a sports jacket that was far too big for him, as though for comic effect. He sat at my table. Then he took out the makings, and began constructing a joint with great devotion and elaboration. Nobody took a blind bit of notice of him except me. I watched him, enjoying the spectacle of someone flagrantly skinning up on licensed premises. He was neither furtive nor exhibitionist about it. Very soon the thing was lit, the makings popped back in his clown's jacket pocket, and the sucking end was being tentatively offered in my direction.

I hesitated. Very often when I'm out and drunk and outside somewhere having a fag, I will accept a proffered joint and take a small puff to be polite. But otherwise I avoid it because it makes me paranoid. And with skunk, I've hit the buffers before I've even passed the thing back. If I'm already drunk, however, the effect is less noticeable and can be overcome by more alcohol if I restrict myself to a polite puff or two.

I was still only halfway down the first pint. The bloke didn't know me from Adam, yet it was kind and sociable of him to include me in his parish. I accepted it, took a drag and passed it on. My phone rang. Trev. 'Where are you, Bud?' The joint came around again. (Again I accepted and then sent it on.) He was in the pub looking for me, he said. I told him I was out the back in the beer garden, and five seconds later Trev appeared: dark-tan brogues, navy-blue Crombie, his blond hair an even one millimetre long all over. He was in ebullient Saturday-night mood, a long glass of house double vodka and lemonade in his hand as if he'd been born with it there. 'Who's the Daddy!' he cried. Then he strode over and made us all budge up so he could sit in among us.

'So what do you all know, then?' said Trev, a vivid, powerful, challenging presence. Trev doesn't smoke pot either normally, and for the same reasons. Also, he holds this particular pub in contempt. It's the one pub in town where anyone with half a brain congregates. In Trev's eyes, the half a brain that these customers have in common is the stupider half. I tend to agree with him. It was a great surprise to see him in here at all.

He gazed around the table taking in each person with a saucy look hoping that someone might reveal a bit of wit or mettle or masculinity. Unfortunately the table had been ambushed by the joint and was completely out of it. They stared back at him: glassy-eyed, speechless, fatuous, paralysed. The bloke in the clown's jacket was totally immobile, like a gonk. No slouch, Trev read the situation comfortably and shook his head sorrowfully, like a headmaster with a row of recidivist infants arraigned before him on the carpet of his office. He turned with mock dread to look at me, saw that I was of the company, and rolled his eyes with bored amusement.

'Come on then, dude,' he said to the bloke in the too big jacket. 'Skin us up another one.' And then he gave a deep sigh of sincere and ineffable boredom.

SIX JAGERBOMBS, PLEASE
30 November 2013

Can it be that the one single agreeable thing about getting old is that one loses one's pot paranoia? No.

I thought I was going to get away with it, but here it came again like a creeping fog: the terrible introspection, the loss of identity, the psychic disintegration, the paranoid delusions. And here already, I noted, was the paralysing delusion that I am rooted to the spot and somehow tied to the company by a bond of loyalty, to the extent that even to uncross my legs and leave the beer-garden table would feel like a terrible betrayal. It's horrible. I hate it.

My immediate task was to try to drink off the paranoia or the evening would be over before it started. Trev was pulling belated, nauseated faces about there being too little or no vodka in his vodka and lemonade. It was supposed to be a double. Canvassing opinion, he gave his glass first to me. I could taste liquefied sweetener with a slice of lemon and nothing else. Here was my chance to pull myself out of this mire, extract myself from the magic circle, and try to retrieve my sense of self before it was chaff in the wind.

I uncrossed my legs, stood up, and — nobody seemed to mind — I went inside to buy a round. The bar was filling rapidly. The pub was small and cosy with a culture of conversation. From a small speaker above my head, the voice and guitar of Muddy Waters competed gently with the murmur of conversation. The bar staff were busy, and looked glad to be doing something at last. I had to stand and wait to be served for what seemed like an eternity.

My usual pot paranoia identity crisis was deepening by the second. If, as some say, the self is ultimately a holding action between competing factions, mine had now gone out for the evening, and the competing factions had decided to throw a party to celebrate, advertised it on Facebook, and 5,000 revellers had turned up and were causing mayhem. And if, as others claim, the self is little more than a social performance, a public role played with lesser or greater competence, I'd got stage fright. I was paralysed. I'd forgotten my lines and forgotten which part I was meant to be playing. I'd even forgotten which play I was in.

I stared at the other customers. This one looked like a collaboration between Alan Ayckbourn and Ionesco. And everyone in the bar was acting their socks off.

The delusions began; the usual delusions; my ordinary neuroses writ large, I think. An unshakable conviction, for example, that these confident, consummate actors gathered here in the bar were operating on a higher plane of consciousness than I was, and that they knew something of crucial importance, perhaps about me, that I cannot imagine nor will ever be permitted to know.

There was not one person in the bar who wasn't engaged in conversation. And yet were not some of these conversations a little studied, I wondered, like those seen over the shoulders of the soap stars in the Rovers Return? I was under furtive scrutiny, there was no doubt about it.

Two could play at that game. I ostentatiously looked through, around, over people: never directly at them. For the benefit of my secret observers, I leant a jaunty elbow on the bar, crossed my legs at the ankles and looked patiently bored (lounge lizard Jeremy). I bent down and affectionately patted the solid flanks of the pub bulldog (Jeremy aka St Francis of Assisi). The dog gave me an offended look and waddled off. I made a great show of studying with fascinated interest the minimalist cartoon of Big Ben on a beer mat (contemporary art connoisseur Jeremy). I checked my iPhone (popular Jeremy) and reread this month's phone bill. I turned and gazed with exaggerated fascination at the glamorous kaleidoscope of glass and mirrors, lights and coloured liquids behind the bar (delightfully childlike Jeremy).

And now the accusations started. I've been ham acting like this all my life. I am a man without a convincing character of his own. A fake. Not once in the past ten years have I ever told the truth for the truth's sake, without calculating the capital that came with it. Not once have I laughed an innocent laugh. I was ugly yet vain, cretinous yet complex. A shirker. An alcoholic. A failure. My existence on earth could be summed up by the single image of a man bent over a bin scraping furiously at a blackened piece of toast with a knife.

'Can I help?' At last, the cheerful face of a bar woman. A mask, of course. But a bloody good one. 'Six Jägerbombs, please, love,' I said. 'And a tray.

BEAR HUNT
14 December 2013

Christmas shopping in Waterstones, I came across a memory card game called *We're Going on a Bear Hunt.* I snatched it up and almost ran with it to the till, where I paid the woman with the smug attitude of a connoisseur. If I'd had a cavalry moustache, I'd have twirled the ends. I'd intended wrapping it up and putting it in my grandson Oscar's stocking, but the wait would have been unbearable. So when I got home, solemn with excitement, I simply handed it to him, and we cleared the decks immediately to play, with Grandad still buttoned into his overcoat.

Do you know the book *We're Going on a Bear Hunt*? No? You haven't lived. The grandson and me, we read a lot. We are working our way through the entire literary canon for the under-fours: *Hairy Maclary from Donaldson's Dairy*; *Katie Morag Delivers the Mail*; *Ruby Flew Too!*; *On the Way Home*; *Owl Babies*; *The Gruffalo*; *The Day Louis Got Eaten.* And of all of them, our all-time favourite is *We're Going on a Bear Hunt.*

A young family — Mum, Dad, the kids, the collie — leave home and go on a bear hunt. 'We're going on a bear hunt,' they sing, in case they forget. 'We're going to catch a big one. It's a beautiful day! We're not scared!' Along the way they meet obstacles: tall grass ('Swishy swashy!'), a chest-deep river (Splash splosh!), a muddy estuary (Squelch squerch!), a dark forest (Stumble trip!). Finally they arrive at the entrance to a bear cave. Suddenly no longer quite as blasé as they were before about hunting bears, they tiptoe into the cave, where, at the far end, they encounter an enormous bear just woken up. 'It's a bear!' yells the panic-stricken family.

It's a terrifying moment. In fact, the encounter with the bear in his cave is so hair-raising that we can't bring ourselves to actually look at it. The bear's surprised, angry face is just too awful. We manage to read on only by carefully turning over two pages at once. The horror continues, increases even, but never again, fortunately, does the angry bear loom so frighteningly large on the page.

The family run for their lives. The furious bear chases them back across flowing river and estuary mud, through tall grass and dark forest. The bear is gaining on them with every turn of the page. The family reach their front door in the nick of time, slamming it in the bear's face, which is visible through the square glass panes. It takes the children's combined strength to prevent the bear from breaking the door in. Finally, the family race upstairs and they all dive under a big pink duvet. Huddled in terror beneath this duvet, they promise each other they will never go on a bear hunt again; the sport is a lot more dangerous than they'd bargained for, presumably.

And that's the end. We always sit there for a few seconds, Oscar and I, absolutely stunned. One of these days, clearly, the bear is going to outstrip the family before they get home and the ensuing carnage will be terrible. We speculate on it. Would the bear eat the entire family or just wantonly kill them? He'd scoff the lot, we think. And would the bear eat the dog too or keep it as a pet? We think eat it as well.

The memory card game based on the book has 54 cards with scenes and characters from the picture book. You lay the cards face-down on your kitchen table and turn up two at a time, remembering which ones were where, endeavouring to make pairs. There are four 'bear' cards, but we make sure we leave those in the box. We don't like to see angry bears, even on memory cards. While we play, I put on carefully chosen background music: Vaughan Williams, perhaps, or The Regimental Band of the Coldstream Guards. We play for hours and hours.

When Oscar wins a pair, which he does about four times as often as his forgetful old Grandad, Oscar does this exultant and rather insane war dance around the table, taunting me. I sit there and take it, loving him. We're friends, he and I. At night, when we've washed our face, he carefully lays his face flannel on mine, symbolising that we are 'best friends', he says. When he grows up, he says, he wants to be a man like me, with glasses. His Mummy and Daddy parted recently, and last week Mummy accidentally swallowed too many headache tablets and had to go to the hospital in an ambulance. He must be glad of a best friend and an exhilarating game of cards at times like these. But no one's been eaten by a bear yet. So all things considered, we're quite lucky really.

LIONS
4 January 2014

I went from the first yoga session of the New Year to the pub. I felt ever so noble. The place was rocking. There was a bloke at the bar looking at his watch, curious as to how long it would take the pill he'd just taken to affect his brain. I was with a woman who kept excusing herself to kiss this other woman. It wasn't snogging exactly. Rather it was miniaturist nibbling and lip-licking. Some tongue, too. But it looked a bit theatrical. Look at us, kind of thing. Were we supposed to be surprised? Aroused? This is an agricultural town. Nobody has batted an eyelid at lesbianism or bisexuality for centuries. If they'd put their backs into it a bit more then, yes, jolly good show, and we might have spectated a bit. In the pub we were drinking gin and tonics and Jägerbombs and Sambuca shots.

When we were properly stoked, we went upstairs to this music joint next door. The band were in full flight, the place was shaking. We pushed our way right to the front, she and I, where the sweaty lead singer got me in a headlock, kissed my ear, put his mouth to it and told me how much he loved me. With malice aforethought I'd brought along some handy pocket-sized tins of gin and tonic to save time queuing at the bar. I cracked them open and gave one to the singer and he downed it in one between verses.

Then this woman and I start busting out our moves. She was a great dancer. A mover. In her spare time she

131

works out, kick-boxes, runs up and down mountains. I'd fancied her for ages but was tongue-tied. She danced against me, simulating sex from the front standing up, then sex from the back. I grabbed her waist and she leaned right back trusting me not to let go. That kind of thing. Then Trev comes dancing over. He's dancing like he's a riding a donkey down a mountainside. He shouts in my ear that he's taken half an e. It was left over from last week, he yells, before I accuse him of selfishness. The woman grabs Trev by the neck and pulls us both in close, like she's a layer of St Ivel between two slices of supermarket bread. Then she gyrates against each of us in turn, showing us her vigorous threesome moves. Impressive they are, too. Never one to miss an opportunity, Trev puts heart and soul into it, as if he's auditioning.

The band was out of this world. Whichever drug of choice was floating boats tonight, the music was lifting all boats on a high spring tide. After a few numbers, the woman calmed down a bit and stopped showing us how energetic and capable she was in the sack. Her head went down, her eyes closed and she slotted into a groove, a good groove, a right groove. But time had speeded up, as it always does. No sooner had we found the groove, than the singer had said, 'Thank you and goodnight!' and he and his band trooped off the stage. The lights came on.

Excusing myself, I went downstairs to smoke a cigarette outside in the street. While I was at it, I went to a cash machine. Sitting on the pavement was a street woman with a shawl over her head. She was surrounded by rubbish bags with clothes in them. I thought she might be begging, but she ignored me. 'What are you doing down there?' I said, tapping in my PIN number. 'I'm a damson in distress,' she said.

Then silence until the machine cleared its throat prior to dispensing my cash. People were spilling out of the music club, shouting and screaming as the fresh air hit. 'I dream about cathedrals,' she said. 'What do you dream about?' 'Lions,' I said. 'Lions prowling on the footpath ahead.' 'Males or females?' she said, interested. 'Both. Would you like a drink?' I said.

She gathered up her things and we went into the pub, which was still serving drinks. At the bar, while we waited for our drinks to come, she told me she'd renounced everything except the world, the flesh and the Devil. But once she had a pint in her hand she didn't want to know me. She pointedly turned her back and went to sit with a friend, a smoke-blackened young man with a tidy whippet lurcher.

I retrieved my yoga mat from behind the bar and carried it and my pint out to the beer garden, where I got involved with an entirely new set of people who invited me to a party. And that's how I went to my first party of the New Year, with a fag in my mouth and my rolled-up yoga mat under my arm.

MALAMATIYYA
11 January 2014

So I go to the all-night house party with my rolled-up yoga mat under my arm. Nice house, middle-class crowd, everybody drunk. Women's screams coming from upstairs. Looking for the lavatory, I find one vacant at the top of the stairs. I'm in mid-stream when this bloke bursts in and slams the door again behind him. He's a big bloke and it's a small lavatory. To accommodate him, I shuffle around the bowl and come at it now from the side. 'Don't mind me, pal,' he says, all business-like. He delicately opens a tiny plastic bag, licks his thumb and shoves it into the powder as if it's sherbert and he's ten years old. He licks his thumb lovingly and plunges it into the bag again. 'Here you go,' he says, and he offers me his white MDMA-coated thumb to suck. 'The Yorkshire method, pal. E by gum.'

He stands his thumb up in front of my face. I hesitate. I've never sucked a man's thumb before. It seems indecent and more to the point terribly unhygienic. Apart from being in his mouth just now, that thumb might have been anywhere since he last washed his hands. 'No, thanks,' I tell him. 'You have that.' But the huge, coated thumb in front of my face is obdurate, unwavering. 'Come on, pal,' he says, with genial condescension. 'It'll put hairs on your chest.'

I transfer my eyes from the bowl to the bulbous thumb in front of my face. If the police were to burst in now, technically I could get seven years for the privilege of leaning forward and sucking his class A off that. This is a casual observation merely, and not a cavil. I look him in the face. One of Boris's bottom 16 per cent of the species with an IQ below 86, I guess, and not looking his best, either. Trying to keep my aim true, I shake my head briskly at the thumb. 'Suit yourself, pal,' he says huffily, and wrestles and barges his way back out of the door with his thumb in his mouth like a baby.

I follow him out and wander around upstairs, looking in the bedrooms, which are all full of drink- and drug-crazed people, trying to find someone I know. In the last bedroom I try, I am successful. There's a woman in the bed and Trev, naked from the waist down, is leaning out of the window smoking a contemplative cigarette.

I have recently become interested in a venerable and extreme branch of Sufism whose adherents call themselves Malamatiyya. Malama is the Arabic word for 'to blame'. The Malamatiyya believe that the root of all evil is the ego or lower self, which they call the nafs. For these austere gentlemen, to be esteemed by others for virtuousness is sinful because it puffs up the nafs. They therefore practise their asceticism in secret, while in public committing the most outrageous acts of impropriety. The public odium they draw down on themselves thus thwarts the nafs and sanctifies them. One of the most revered Malamatiyya saints used to horrify his followers by whipping out his penis and urinating indiscriminately in the street. And I am lately beginning to suspect Trev of secretly being a Malamatiyya holy man. A nicer person you couldn't hope to meet. But the behaviour is consistently egregious. Adherence to this esoteric Sufi doctrine is the only way to explain him. 'All right, dude?' he says.

Hours later we leave the party together and head back to his place. I've remembered my yoga mat and have it tucked safely under my arm. On the way, we pass a house with lights still on upstairs and down. An old flame of Trev lives there, and he motions that he wants to call in. It's about six o'clock in the morning.

And this is how drunk we both are. There's no doorbell so he must knock on the door. But neither of us can manage one decent knock between us. It's a feat of manual dexterity beyond our capability. Trev's hand misses the door completely at the first attempt. In subsequent attempts, his hand is too flaccid to form a fist and he merely caresses the door with the back of his hand and he topples sideways. Even when bracing himself against me, his hand crumples like tissue paper against the glass and slides off without a sound. Neither of us can speak. I am unwilling to take my hands out of my pockets in case I fall down. I stand there patiently, like a cow, with my yoga mat tucked firmly under my arms.

And then I have a bright idea. I meticulously unroll my yoga mat in the postage stamp of the front garden and lay down on it in the corpse pose while Trev keeps trying.

BO
1 February 2014

I shifted a chest of drawers that hadn't been moved for years, and found an old photograph lying among the dust and the cobwebs behind it. I picked it up and studied it, fascinated by the alien light of the mid-1980s. A summer meadow. A terrier ring at a dog and ferret show. And there I am, a stranger to my present self, crouching beside a tidy Jack Russell terrier bitch. She has liquid, almond-shaped eyes set in a black-and-tan face. The well-proportioned body is piebald black and white. Smooth coated. Her tail is undocked, the blood-blackened bone showing through the sparse white hairs at the tip. She is looking with calm, confident interest at something off-camera.

People often commented on what they saw as kindness in her face. My mother often expressed the far-fetched belief that she was a Christian. Indoors, she had perfect good manners. She was sensitive and you could command her with your eyes. The day I met her, she jumped up on my lap and I immediately picked her up and flung her away. I was used to Alsatians and was stupidly contemptuous of the little dog. She never asked to come up on my lap again. She was quiet and watchful and careful not to get under anyone's feet. She never asked for food, though thirst would drive her to bark at the kitchen tap. She was fastidious as a cat in her cleanliness and when doing her business. She had one terrible, overriding, maniacal vice, however. She lived to kill.

My brother-in-law got her from a Dartmoor farmer who had found her out foraging alone. My brother-in-law gave her to my brother and my brother gave her to me. Then, she looked about three years old. The first time I took her for a walk she killed a rat right in front of me. She chased it twice around a telegraph pole, caught it with a twisting leap, shook it to death, cast the corpse aside, then jogged on as if nothing had happened. Snuff ballet. From start to finish about two seconds. I'd never seen a terrier nail a rat before and I was astonished and impressed.

But a rat was nothing. Her bread and butter, or so she thought, was badger. In the early days of our acquaintance, I spent a lot of time lying on the ground with my head as far down a badger hole as it would go, shouting myself hoarse, anxiously alive to the fact that the fine for disturbing a badger set was £2,000. Whether she was what a badger-digger would call 'self-entering' or whether she had been carefully trained, it was impossible to know. But she was the consummate badger-digger's dog. Once she'd found a badger deep in his set, she'd bark excitedly in its face all afternoon, presumably in the mistaken belief that I would shortly be digging quickly and illegally down to the rumpus in order to put a violent end to Mr Brock's life.

We couldn't go on like that. So on our walks we tried to forget Piggy and concentrate our minds instead on bushing bunny rabbits in the gorse. She took to it. She had no deft killing technique with a rabbit and it was best all round and saved time if I did the despatching for her. It wasn't the catching them that was difficult, it was lugging the bloody things home afterwards. She carried her tail like a flagpole and the tip became shredded by thorns and gorse needles and bled so copiously that she would be covered in her own blood. Her ears tore and bled easily too. No wonder they used to crop ears as well as the tail in the old days. About once a week I'd have a careful look under her thin coat and extract any tics using the burning tip of a roll-up and tweezers.

For several years I spent all of my spare time in her company catching rabbits on long walks. She was a proper earth dog, though. An indefatigable tunneller drawn irresistibly to badger sets. Bushing rabbits above ground, though it satisfied her desire to kill, was in all conscience a sinful waste of her talents. One sunny day an adder bit her in the armpit and she succumbed to the venom aged about seven.

We called her Bo. I must have shouted that name down badger holes a million times. Knowing that bitch terrier was one of the joys of my life. I studied the photograph and wondered with shame how I had failed to think of her lately, and how I had become estranged from the person crouching next to her. To make small amends, I put the photograph in a little tin frame and put it on the mantelpiece.

CHEZ BROWN
EAGLE FEATHER
5 February 2014

'I'm wasted,' said Trev, meaning not that his life is futile, but that his mind was overwhelmed by illegal drugs. He conceded it. It wasn't often that drugs ruined him, but tonight they had, and credit where credit's due.

We were a disparate post-pub gathering of about a dozen people. At a push you might call it a party. The house was small, the party confined to a brightly lit kitchen and a square, semi-dark living room. Everyone bar me was in the kitchen doing this, that and the other. I was standing in the darkness of the living room listening to Hawkwind on the CD player and thinking that surely they were the greatest band in the world, ever. Then Trev came in from the kitchen with this latest report on the state of his mind.

He placed his hands on my shoulders and made a speech. 'You, bud,' he said, 'are one great man. You put me to shame. I stand before you now ashamed because I'm not one tenth of the man you are. I'm glad to know you, bud. You are quality. Come here.' Then he waved me towards him, inviting me to give him a man hug. So I stepped forward and tried to encircle him with my arms, but they were too short for the job. And we stood there like that, in the semi-darkness, with Hawkwind forcing the mental pace. And then he released me, regarded me solemnly, and returned to the kitchen. He must have been very wasted indeed.

And then another, different figure entered the room. Although the company was small, and I had been there for hours, I hadn't so far managed to speak to anybody new, or introduce myself, or even to find out whose home this was. (I'd followed the crowd there unquestioningly.) I was enjoying a rare holiday from my inner critic, I liked myself for once, I just didn't feel much like saying anything. Words seemed otiose and inadequate. 'That for which we find words is already dead in our hearts,' said Nietzsche. 'There is always a kind of contempt in the act of speaking.' It was sort of like that. Sometimes I danced, sometimes I stood licking my lips to the music, which seemed acceptable in that house. Not speaking and licking one's lips was something understood there.

Then this other bloke came in and urged me to grip his hand with an arm wrestling-type clasp as a sign of his brotherly love. He was bald except for a Mohican strip of hair of the spectacular kind that one still sees on postcards with a quaintly anachronistic 'swinging London' theme. His name was Brown Eagle Feather, he said, and he followed the way of the shaman. He'd been on week-long courses in Brighton and elsewhere and his training had taught him to be sensitive to a person's spirit. And he wanted to say that I was one cool guy. He didn't know who I was. He hadn't met me before. I had hardly said a word. But I gave off a good 'vibe'. I had a cool spirit. This wasn't his house. This was the house of the woman he loved, the woman who had changed his life for good. So he just wanted to say, on behalf of them both, that I was welcome. Then we did another hand clasp thing and he went out.

They must have been talking about me with approval in the kitchen because next a man with bare arms, mascara, a slit skirt and black tights came in and asked me did I want a blow job. It would the best one I had ever had, he could guarantee it. Did I want to go kayaking with him, then? He'd love to take me down the river. He was a kayaking instructor. He bent an arm at the elbow and showed me a bicep, clearly a work in progress. Then he went out, glancing coquettishly at me over his shoulder as he passed through the doorway.

Next Trev came in accompanied by the love of Brown Eagle Feather's life, a pleasant, homely-looking sort. She went to the CD player and put on 'Samba Pa Ti' by Santana and she hung off his neck and they danced together very slowly and very sensuously. They invited me to join them and we formed a slowly revolving circle of love.

Then everyone in the kitchen suddenly migrated to the living room, filling it. It was like an exodus. Someone switched the light on. Brown Eagle Feather tapped me on the shoulder. He looked tragic. 'Excuse me, man,' he said. 'Have you got anything?' 'I'm afraid not,' I said, licking my lips. He couldn't have looked more crestfallen if his crest had indeed collapsed. 'Okay. Cool, man,' he said.

BREED
8 February 2014

My first ride in a stretch Hummer. I haven't lived, I now realise. The prodigious, ridiculous thing, tricked out in multicoloured neon piping, drew up outside the pub where we were getting stoked. I was privileged to be invited by Trev to his niece's 18th birthday celebration in a nightclub. It was very much a family affair and they are a proud family. 'Who the fuck is that?' I kept hearing from the younger, micro-skirted, six-inch-heeled element, in disgusted tones, referring to me, and Trev would do his best to explain me to them.

Trev thought a 'punch-up' inevitable when we got to the club. The women were as liable to start one as the men, in his opinion. I looked around at the state of play as we waited to climb aboard the limo. One of the young nephews was already being strenuously argued out of having a warm-up fight with some innocent and surprised-looking bystander. With one exception, the younger women were drunk in the same squiffy, deliberately vacuous way, and teetering about precariously on their tall heels as though on stilts. The exception was passed out lopsidedly on a chair. The birthday girl's proud father, emerging from the pub to see his princess for the day climb into her smoked-glass carriage, fell down backwards twice in the space of five seconds.

But the most likely instigator of a punch-up, to anyone who knew their history, was a nephew of Trev called

Danny, not often seen out much these days, late thirties, wiry build, big blond hair, and tonight wearing a T-shirt with the single word 'Breed' across his chest. Looking about him and rubbing his hands together in delighted anticipation, he said to me, 'Well, I don't know about you, but I'm all ready for a spot of fudge-packing, Jer.'

We clambered aboard the limo. Thumping music, disco lights, mirrored bar. I admit it — I felt like a lord. At the front, the birthday girl and her pals screamed for drinks and danced crazily in their seats. The driver appeared at the open door. I was beginning to forget what a sober person looked like. He wasn't going to let us have any booze, he said, because our young ladies were out of control. So we elder statesmen at the back assured him we would keep an eye on them, and he handed in two very cheap-looking bottles of sparkling rosé, reluctantly, as if it was against his better judgment.

The ride took about 20 minutes. I sat beside a bloke whose shaved head had what looked like an old sabre cut running obliquely across it. Duffle-coat toggle stuck through an earlobe. He sat clutching his empty glass flute between his legs and stared grimly ahead. He and I were the quiet corner. He spoke to me just once on the journey. After about ten minutes he turned to me and said, 'I'm dying for a piss.' And that was it.

Our stretched Hummer pulled up outside the club and we decanted. The birthday girl teetered on her high heels, grabbed at one of her pals' arms to stop herself falling, and three of them went down on the wet tarmac like skittles. It was now midnight. Taxis from all over mid-Devon queued to deposit their inebriated contents then sped away. The cold night air was making already drunk people suddenly much drunker and a hellish sort of pandemonium reigned outside the club. We formed up and joined the queue to go in. Somewhere up ahead I heard Danny announce to the world, 'I'm rolling back the years!'

It was two quid each to get in. There must have been 700 or 800 people inside. Perhaps 200 of these were besieging a long bar manned by four or five bar staff. I tried but it was hopeless. Looking around, I noticed a smoking area through a swinging door. Smokers were packed in there like commuters on the Central line. As I watched, a disturbance erupted in their midst. Savage punches were being thrown in the unlikeliest directions. Screaming. At the epicentre, the blond head of Danny was jerking about as though he were riding a bucking bronco. Bouncers streamed past me. A minute later, they were marching Danny out through a fire exit with our young ladies tottering precariously along behind, yelling abuse in their ears.

Two others of our party (chaps) were thrown out also, and with no one left to talk to I went outside too. Trev was patiently reasoning with his nephew Danny, who was arguing for bloody vengeance. Our young ladies were sitting on the wet tarmac disconsolate. It was decided we might as well all go home again. 'Sorry, Jer,' said Danny when he saw that I'd come out too. 'Don't apologise!' I said. 'We'd have all died of thirst in there anyway.'

MISSING IAN
15 February 2014

Every time I hear that song 'Sex & Drugs & Rock & Roll' played on the radio, I think, Lord, how I miss Ian Dury. Then I wish they'd play something other than that plodder, especially when there are so many great songs of his to choose from. Some people knew all the words to Dark Side of the Moon; others to Sergeant Pepper; but we knew all the words to New Boots and Panties!!. And what words! He was our poet laureate. Put that record on and everybody would sing their heads off, especially to 'Billericay Dickie'. 'I bought a lot of brandy/ when I was courting Sandy/ took eight to make her randy/ and all I had was shandy/ another thing with Sandy/ what often came in handy/ was passing her a 'Mandy'/ she didn't half go bandy.' I recognised the hilarious Saturday-night music-hall qualities in a song like 'Billericay Dickey', but at 18 I also thought those lyrics were philosophy. The man was a hero to us.

Twenty years later I went with him to Zambia. He had cancer by then and had put on weight. He went there to publicise a polio vaccination campaign and I was one of the journalists sent to write it up. I couldn't believe that I was even on the same plane as Ian Dury, let alone that I would get to swap pleasantries with the guy for nearly a week. After we'd spoken a few times, he couldn't believe it, either, that a bloke like me wrote for the Sunday Telegraph. He thought someone was pulling his leg.

At the Zambian immigration desk there was a delay because his entry visa wasn't in order, and there was a further delay because he offered the official a bribe to forget about it, and the official had taken offence and made a scene. 'I thought slipping the geezer a cockle would do the trick,' he explained to me in all innocence afterwards. A cockle is ten pounds. Cockle = cock and hen = ten = a tenner.

Ian had a minder with him called Derek the Draw. Derek the Draw's main job was to set Ian on his feet again whenever his boss, who was disabled by polio, fell over. Sometimes Ian crumpled unexpectedly and Derek would have him back up on his feet in a flash — years of practice and technique, I suppose — without fuss or embarrassment. Derek the Draw was a big, gentle bloke, with a calm, humorous intensity filtering out of the gaps between the long hair, wild beard and droopy moustache. He loved Ian like a brother and was very far from the type of person one normally associates with the word 'minder'. We were in a bar in Lusaka and Ian said to Derek, 'Give us a tune, Del.' And Derek the Draw went and got his guitar and played it, leaning far back on his bar stool until he was almost horizontal, and he was the most fantastic guitar picker I'd ever seen.

But before that I'd undergone the thrilling ordeal, on our first night in Zambia, of being invited up to Ian and Derek's modest hotel room for a 'nightcap'. Ian had brought a wind-up radio with him. The technology was in its infancy then. And he, Derek the Draw and I listened to a local African pop station on this wind-up radio and passed joints back and forth while Ian gave us his random thoughts. I can't remember any of them, but I thought

I'd died and gone to heaven. I offered to be the wind-up person, but Ian was very possessive of his radio and insisted on that job, and he put it under his arm and wound it lovingly.

Then he said to me, as if he'd been meaning to say it for a long time and had been putting it off: 'What do you fucking look like?' 'What?' I said. 'You've got to learn to dress yourself, Jel,' he said beseechingly. 'You can't even tie a tie, you nit.' So he stood up and made me stand up and he retied my tie in a Windsor knot. Then he said, 'You've got to get a hat, my son. Walk into a room with a hat on and every bird in the room is going to turn round and clock you. If you want to get head [sic], get a hat. Try this one.' And he positioned a Lock and Company white linen 'Florida' bowling hat on my head and carefully adjusted the angle. Then he took it off again and wrote on the inside: 'Oi, Jel, where's my fucking hat?' A generous, very human man, as well as a great lyricist, Ian Dury was. And I still miss him.

HOPING FOR
A CONTINUANCE
8 March 2014

I've had a medical procedure that is 'likely' to leave me impotent. A nurse is coming around dishing out Tramadol, a painkiller of the morphine family. I raise my hand smartly. She steers her drugs trolley towards me and my bed in the corner of the six-bed male ward. 'Are you in pain, Mr Clarke?' 'Absolute agony,' I say. I'm looking fetching in a pair of white, knee-length tights. I'm hooked up to a drip to put fluids in, and catheterised to take them away. This thickness of the catheter tube and the site of its emergence is hard to credit at first. The fluid in the collection bag looks mostly like blood. I've lost all feeling from the waist down. But I'm not in pain. On the contrary I feel quite magnificent. The residue of the Rohypnol I was given this morning to sedate me, plus the continued effects of an epidural, have made pain a distant memory. I'm just being greedy, that's all.

The nurse glances at my notes and dismisses my application with an irritated wave. The bloke in the bed opposite, on the other hand, is in so much pain he is allowed to decide his own dosage. He thinks two tablets. Men in hospital wards have a uniformly vagrant air, irrespective of their social class. The tousled hair, the five o'clock shadow, the ill-fitting gown, the public sleeping. I suspect this man of being middle class, however. He reads, for one thing, unlike the rest of us, and with great attention, especially to his magazine, which doesn't have photos in it. I mark him down as the Senior British Officer.

The man in the bed beside his is, I think, working class. It's something about the unending virtuosity and evangelical fervour of his farting and burping, and the pleasant sociability with which he addresses the nurses, tea ladies, cleaners and other untouchables who like to stop by and pass the time of day with him.

The man occupying the bed beside mine reminds me visually and spiritually of the actor Roy Kinnear. He walks about the ward with his gown untied and open at the back. Walking towards you he looks decently clothed; walking away entirely naked. I heard him tell our wind man that he works for the government, but refused to elaborate when pressed, conceding only that he worked for the 'nice side'.

The nurse assigned to us is exceedingly kind but almost belligerently gay. Andrew calls me Mr Clarke as he tenderly checks my buttocks for pressure sores. I object. My name's Jel, I say. Call me Jel. 'Jel!' he says, standing and straightening himself the better to absorb this strange news. He carefully enunciates the single syllable. 'How so? Do tell!' I tell him how it is common where I come from to take the initial of the Christian name and add '-el' for an easy nickname. Southend is rife with Tels, Dels and Mels, I tell him. 'My name's Jeremy — hence, Jel,' I say, concluding my exposition on a triumphant note. He looks doubtful. He says the rule wouldn't work in his case because his name begins with a vowel. 'But you could be Anel!' I say, thrilled for him. 'I don't think we'll go there — Jel,' he says archly.

That was the early afternoon. For the rest of the day I lay there while the drugs and the novelty wore off and the feeling gradually returned to my lower half. Sometimes the bed curtain was drawn back and I could sit and observe the excruciating agonies of the Senior British Officer. Even turning a page made him wince. At other times my curtain was drawn, and I sat and studied the washed-out pattern of famous London landmarks. During the afternoon, each of the other three men on the ward was visited by his partner: all of them wives, I think. The Senior British Officer was suddenly amazingly cheerful and wreathed in smiles, his pain forgotten. At his wife's appearance, Roy Kinnear's condition deteriorated dramatically (I thought he was going to die), but it revived again the moment she left. While over in the other corner the wind thankfully dropped completely for the duration of visiting hours.

And then tea was dished up and taken away, and the lights were turned out, and we were put to bed like chickens. Roy Kinnear had a terribly disturbed night, making extraordinary noises as nightmare succeeded nightmare. First he was aggressively citing an imaginary bull to charge at him. Then he was teetering dangerously on a high wire. Then he was having a shuddering orgasm. Then he was barking out orders on a parade ground. And then I, too, fell asleep, ending my first day, hoping and praying for a continuance of potency.

KEEP DRINKING
MR CLARKE!
15 March 2014

The catheter stung exquisitely when I lay down. So I stood up. All night I stood by my hospital bed, tethered by my penis to the transparent collection bag hanging off the bed rail, reading Artemis Cooper's life of Patrick Leigh Fermor. In 1931, not knowing what to do with himself, Paddy walked to Constantinople, as he called it. I rested the paperback on my pillow under the spotlight and walked with him across Europe, much of it still feudal.

Our hero had just emerged from a hayrick after having a spontaneous foursome with his Serbian girlfriend and two Hungarian peasant girls they had met in a field, when I made a startling and revolutionising discovery.

For the past 12 hours I'd been labouring under the false belief that the catheter bag was fixed immovably to the bed rail, and that the two feet of clear tubing from me to it were a kind of punitive leash. But at around three in the morning, irritated enough by the catheter's painful restrictions to bend down for a closer look, I realised that the blood-filled bag was merely suspended from the rail by a hook, and could be detached by merely lifting it with an outstretched forefinger, and could be walked around with, like an outré handbag, even as far as Constantinople if needs be. (Though it would have been a damned nuisance in hayricks with Hungarian peasant women.)

It was a moment of liberation. I picked up my bag and went for an early morning stroll around the ward. Twenty-eight male patients were asleep in three dormitories. The noise! It was like Romford market on a Saturday morning. There were snorers and grunters, and groaners and babblers, and wailers and moaners, and even a demented shouter. Each bed bay was dimly and eerily lit, so I might have been wandering among the gruesome exhibits of a waxworks museum, with exaggerated sound effects played on a loop.

On the way round I met one of the night nurses, an affable, brisk Chinese woman. 'Good evening, Mr Clarke!' she said, delighted to see me up and about, even at that hour. She couldn't stop. But in passing she briefly narrowed her eyes at the contents of my bag. It was full — about a litre of what looked to me like blood. But where I saw blood, she saw cause for congratulation. 'Oh, well done!' she said. And it occurred to me how one is extravagantly praised for excreta both at the beginning of life and towards the end. She urged me to keep up the good work by drinking plenty of water. If I did that, she promised that I would be rewarded at lunchtime with my release papers.

Before she went off duty, she came to my bed, where I was back reading standing up, and she made me sit. Then, in a strangely intimate moment, she slowly but steadily withdrew the catheter from my bladder and finally right out, while my eyeballs started from their sockets. Then I leapt off the bed, bent double with my hands between my thighs, and bowed repeatedly to her, laughing with shock and relief. She laughed. As she exited through my curtain she said brightly, 'Keep drinking, Mr Clarke.' Still grimacing, I solemnly assured her that I would do my best.

In the morning, her cheerful republican regime handed over the governance of our ward to an energetic dictatorship. In a whirl of activity, beds were made, pills issued, menu cards filled in, floors mopped and stools voided and sent off by express delivery for detailed analysis by someone who is presumably glad to have a job at all. Breakfast (cereal and something akin to toast) was eaten and cleared. Two brown-coated technicians came and screwed the bracket of my spotlight more securely to the wall. A raven-haired volunteer pensioner in fluorescent orange trainers pushing a trolley offered tea and coffee and double cream in the coffee. A junior doctor appeared at the foot of my bed along with a large retinue of completely unserious medical students who crowded round. She too told me I must keep drinking. I said I liked her shirt. From the bed on the other side of the curtain came a sustained, single-note, methane-driven vibrato, concluding with a flourish on a rising Australian interrogative.

When the dust had finally settled on all of that, I was handed a cardboard receptacle and told that my commission was to fill it three times with urine, after which I would be allowed home. I assured the nurse that it would be a piece of piss. Then I settled down with Patrick Leigh Fermor's extraordinary progress across Mitteleuropa in one hand, and a plastic hospital tumbler filled with water on the other, and set about its conversion.

DAD! DAD!
22 March 2014

My brother's three Borders are called Roxy, Ruby and Taz. My one ambition in life is to own a terrier again, or rather three terrier bitches, just so that I can call them Tray, Blanch and Sweetheart. (Lear, mad on the heath: 'The little dogs and all, Tray, Blanch and Sweetheart, see, they bark at me.') I ask my brother for the latest news of his dogs.

He says he recently took Ruby up to Yorkshire, to be served by a well-known pedigree Border stud dog. My brother is a regular customer there. It's a ten-hour round trip. The moment he draws up in his car, he says, the dog's owner comes out into the yard and unrolls his 'mating mat' and lays it down, and his stud dog goes ballistic with joy, knowing what's in store. Then my brother gets Ruby out of the car and sets her on the mat, and the owner releases the dog, who is across that yard like an arrow and starts the job without so much as a 'how-do-you-do'.

When the dogs have tied, the dog's owner invites my brother into his kitchen and puts the kettle on. Here they have the same conversation that they have every time my brother goes up there. It's about a Hoopoe. This man loves birds, and the annual visit of our most exotic visitor to his garden is the highlight of his year. The man has a thick, dialect-rich Yorkshire accent, and my brother is a wonderful mimic. And my brother has me in paroxysms with his rendition of the man's excited account of the comings and goings of 'Th'oopoe', while the dogs are coupling on the mat in the yard.

Then we talk football. Or more specifically football chants. Yesterday he emailed over a Daily Mirror chart of the top ten best chants from the past decade. We discuss it. I argue that the Manchester United fans singing to Luis Suárez: 'Your teeth are offside, your teeth are offside, Luis Suárez your teeth are offside' is the funniest song, in spite of being undeservedly well down the list. My brother says that the Mirror illustrated the article with a photograph of Luis Suárez's teeth. Not his face, just the teeth caught at a goofy moment. And then my brother sticks out his upper front teeth as far as they will go, and looks at me, and he looks so ridiculous (bearing in mind that he spends most of his week as a big, incorruptible policeman, who, on an uncompromising point of principle, nicks anyone who calls him a pig, or who even makes a sotto voce noise like a pig as he passes by in the high street) that I laugh at him until he dissolves in my tears.

Number one on the list was West Ham fans singing 'His name is Rio and he watches from the stand' — to the tune of 'Rio' by Duran Duran. This might not sound remotely amusing printed here like this in a Spectator column. And perhaps it isn't. But somehow it was irresistibly funny to us at that moment as we sang it together. So funny that neither of us could finish it, both of us being Hammers fans, who can easily picture Rio Ferdinand's protruding, disconsolate lower lip, and we were both helpless.

Then my brother told me that he had recently achieved his ambition to play for 90 minutes in the same Sunday side as his son. His son is 16 and a promising midfielder; my brother is 47. He tells me how he loves to hear his son screaming dementedly at him for the ball, going, 'Dad! Dad!' When they first hear it, he says, the opposing team can't run for laughing, and from that moment on, whenever he gets the ball, everyone on the pitch yells, 'Dad! Dad!' at him.

I love my brother. He never gossips or shows the slightest interest in the wider family politics. He just does his job as well as he can, and does his best for his family, and keeps himself fit with football and judo, and his dogs fit with long and varied walks. The last time he took Roxy to the vet, her pulse was so slow that the vet took five minutes to find one.

And now he's pushing out his Luis Suárez teeth at me again as we drive across the tawny barrenness of central Dartmoor, gilded now with early morning sunshine. We have hot coffee, and fresh crusty rolls filled with cold roast beef and horseradish, and satsumas in our daypacks. Roxy, Ruby and Taz are in the boot, softly whimpering their anticipation. And my brother and I have the entire day ahead of us to disappear into the cathedral silence and walk and talk and laugh. His idea. To get me out and about again, he says.

YOUNG LOVE
29 March 2014

Another sunny Sunday morning and the phone rings. I pick up the receiver. It's Frank. I groan inwardly. Frank is a doctor and an old family friend and a great talker. What he has to say is always intelligent and interesting and often funny. He will explain scientific laws or philosophical arguments or biological functions with elaborate care and in the simplest possible terms, so that even a child might understand them. My immune system, for example, is run by soldiers with powers of arrest and internment, constantly on high alert for terrorists. His talk is invariably sprinkled with his favourite Jewish jokes, and bawdy songs, which he breaks into with little or no provocation, his cherubic face aglow with pleasure. But he has zero emotional intelligence and his talk is always delivered In the form of an interminable and exhausting monologue.

So on this sunny spring Sunday morning with the primroses out and grass to be mown, he's the last person I want to talk to. But it's been a while. And in the fast lane of the local pool earlier something in my knee went twang! and I'm crippled. So I take my mug of coffee and do a choreographed fall into the nearest chair and resign myself to being subjected to a Frank monologue.

He'd been to Cambodia with a party of doctors on a fact-finding tour. Goodness, those Cambodian women! They had to be seen to be believed. As the doctors were strolling together in the town, one of the women doctors had teased him by saying, 'Gee, Frank, I don't know how you can resist all these fabulous women.' Frank replied that he woke up every morning wondering the same thing. But in truth he hadn't been resisting them at all. In fact, he'd been conducting his own independent fact-finding tour from the moment he'd stepped off the plane.

His approach was capricious rather than systematic, by the sound of it. Instead of heading for the bars, like any normal monger looking for local colour, he patrolled the outdoor markets, imagining presumably that every Cambodian woman he saw was a possibility. Which seems a trifle arrogant and wholly misguided to me. But I don't cavil, partly because one doesn't interrupt Frank when he's in full flow, and partly because he had a tremendous success almost right away.

He had his sights set on this one particular 'gorgeous piece of ass' in a shop. I forget what sort of a shop he said it was, but in Frank went, no doubt muttering 'Ding dong!' under his breath, making a beeline for this exceptionally alluring 'ass'. In the course of giving this woman the Frank seduction chat, he made his profession known and word quickly spread that there was a doctor in the house. And before he knew it, he was inundated with the unwell and conducting an afternoon surgery on a first-come-first-served basis. They were queuing out of the door. A woman kindly came in from the shop next door and offered to act as his interpreter. Her name was Ian. She wasn't bad-looking either. Between consultations they chatted. She worked part-time in the shop next door and part-time at the temple. She wasn't paid for either work. She did it for love. It was this simple statement, said Frank, suddenly hoarse with solemnity, that made him fall in love with Ian on the spot. It was the meeting of two humanitarian minds.

She took him to meet her parents. They were simple rice farmers. They lived in a one-room hut with no furniture and at meal times they squatted on the concrete floor to eat. Water was ladled out of a bucket. Everything was spotlessly clean. Nobody drank straight from the ladle. The intelligent attention to matters of hygiene by these simple peasants left him speechless with admiration. He was invited to sit on the floor and eat. He did so. It all reminded him very much, he says, of his simple cockney childhood. In fact, he felt so overwhelmingly at home there that he asked the father if he could have his daughter's hand in marriage. The father hospitably agreed. And the happy ending is that Frank brought Ian back to England just after Christmas and married her in his local register office. 'I don't know what she sees in me, Jeremy, but we just seem to hit it off so well,' he says. 'How old is Ian, Frank?' I said, mentally bracing myself. She's 28, he says.

Frank is 83. I find myself trembling on the brink of a moral judgment but restrain myself. It would be impossible to get a word in edgeways, anyway. I sip my coffee and look out of the window at the sea, which today is a striking hyacinth shade of blue.

DROIT DE SEIGNEUR
22 April 2014

In my opinion,' says Alistair Webster QC, author of the Liberal Democrats' internal report into Lord Rennard's droit de seigneur-style pulling technique, 'the evidence of behaviour which violated the personal space and autonomy of the complainants was broadly credible.' I'll tell you what behaviour that violates personal space is.

I was on a Nile cruise press trip: Aswan to Luxor. We were three hacks and a woman from the PR company. We'd done Edfu, Kom Ombo, Karnak, Thebes, the Valley of the Kings. In bed at night, if I shut my eyes tightly, I could see hieroglyphics emblazoned on the insides of my eyelids.

Our last night was spent at one of Cairo's better hotels. The other two hacks were abstemious. The PR woman was permanently on duty. Every night had been an early night. I was ready for a good drink and this looked like a good place to have one. We dined with the hotel manager at a table in an enormous banqueting hall of gilt and polished marble.

He sat next to me. He was a courteous, civilised, sceptical man with Cupid's bow lips and a feminine delicacy in the way he held his cigarettes low down between his middle fingers. In both appearance and spirit he reminded me of the Alexandrian poet C.P. Cavafy, of whom I am a devotee. He drank steadily and smoked throughout the five courses, eating little, and his staff attended to him with grave respect, replacing his ashtray with a clean one after each cigarette. His English was perfect and his conversation ranged far and wide. He had tried all the mainstream religions, he said, and believed Hinduism to be the most profound. Tomorrow he was leaving for a week of solitary contemplation in the Sinai desert. While grinning dancers thrust their tasselled bellies at us, he successfully flattered me by listening with concentrated stillness and attentiveness to my glottal-stopped inanities as though I were a Solomon or a Kant.

We talked intensely throughout the meal. The others, after a week in each other's faces, were glad to watch the show. Finally, pushing his dessert bowl wearily aside, he lit yet another cigarette, regarding me with a slightly fatuous glint in his eye. 'But tell me, Jeremy,' he said, 'have you ever made love with a man?'

I was a pretty boy as a teenager and so I was happy to have, and well practised at, the conversation which I now knew was coming up. 'No,' I said. He leant back in his chair, placed a hand over his heart and studied me with patient amusement. 'Why not?' he said. 'Too busy,' I said. 'Come with me to my bed tonight,' he said. 'I have an uninterrupted view of the pyramids, and I will make love to you like you have never been made love to before. I will demonstrate to you, Jeremy, that there is infinitely greater pleasure in making love with a man than with a woman. Come. Please. Open your mind.'

The others, true to form, hared off to their beds as soon as was decently possible. I stayed to drink. I had only to look significantly at a waiter and seconds later another drink would arrive. Marvellous. Meanwhile the manager pleaded, cajoled, insisted, argued, begged and mocked until he became boring about it. Finally he tried subterfuge. 'Come to my office,' he said. 'I have something very interesting to show you.' I scoffed. He held up a hand to bid the universe stop for a moment while he solemnly swore there would be no funny business.

His office was just off the palatial marble foyer. As we went in he slammed the door behind me and launched himself at me. He pinned me against the door with fanatical strength and clamped his cherubic lips on to mine. His strength amazed me, and it took the entirety of mine to prise his face away and then force the rest of him off. And then he came back at me with even greater fury than before and I had to wrestle him to the ground. He fought me every centimetre of the way. He was so strong I wondered whether mine wasn't going to be enough and I'd have to get my thumb in his eye. And then his strength gave out and I got up off the floor and made it through the door. I'd walked perhaps ten yards across the marble to where a concierge was standing behind a desk, when the manager came flying out of his office, slipped over and glided for a good five yards on his shirt front along the marble. I looked at the concierge. He looked back at me as if to say, 'What?'

Now that is having one's personal space violated. It is not, surely, having a hand brush against your leg so lightly that it is uncertain whether it was intended or not.

BABU
29 April 2014

Two years ago, roughly, for a travel piece, I flew to Delhi
and took a southbound train to a dusty railway platform in
Rajasthan. There I was met by a smiling man with a gold
earring who introduced himself as my driver for the week.
His name was Babu. I must be a VIP, he said, because he
was the company's top driver and he always was given the
VIP jobs. From now on, he said, he would be treating me
as his god. Then he said, just to make sure, because there
was no telling these days, and I didn't by any stretch of
the imagination look the part: 'Excuse me, sir, but in your
country are you VIP?' I laughed and said certainly not.
But he seemed to take my laugh and denial as a sign that
perhaps I really might be a VIP. I was English, after all.
And there is no telling with the English and their always
saying one thing and meaning another.

For the next seven days, Babu drove me around
Rajasthan, stopping each night at either a hill fort or a
palace offering B&B, after which he withdrew to more
humble accommodation. In the morning, whatever my
own condition, I'd find him standing beside his washed car
with a loving smile and a smart salute. Our itinerary was
called 'Unknown Rajasthan' and some of it was unknown
even to Babu, who was Rajasthani. It took us away from the
main roads and on to tracks that had been recently washed
away by flash floods. 'Unknown Rajasthan, sir!' Babu would
laugh when he had to resort once again to his map.

A week previously, I'd foolishly talked myself into getting engaged to a woman who clearly didn't like me. And I was jet-lagged. So I was numbed and preoccupied and I didn't speak much. I just looked out of the rear window at passing rural Rajasthan — which can perhaps be best summed up as colourful feudalism with electricity pylons. And then I got tired of being thrown around in the back of Babu's car on the rough roads, and I bought a sticky black opium ball to cheer myself up. I think Babu enjoyed my princely, opiated taciturnity, seeing it as an encouraging sign that I was well used to being driven, and was probably therefore a genuine VIP. He drove with a ramrod-straight back and his hands on the steering wheel at ten to four, and he looked ahead with utmost vigilance and commitment to our cause. He spoke only when spoken to, or to offer refreshment. He also advised me about the right amount of opium to break off and swallow at a time. ('No, no, sir! Half, sir! Half!')

After we'd been going for a couple of days, the amazing beauty of the Rajasthani women began to register on me enough for me to comment excitedly to Babu about it. This led to conversation breaking out between us. Even the women on the road-mending gangs were breathtaking. He was reluctant at first to bandy opinions with his god, but my enthusiasm stirred his local patriotism. 'Very beautiful, very hard-working, sir. In Rajasthan, if you have strong penis you can get a lot of lady, sir.'

I told him about my insane engagement, concluding that I would much rather come and live in Rajasthan and marry a road mender. Babu thought this an excellent idea. 'Not one, sir,' he admonished. 'Two.' To ascertain whether in fact two would be best, or whether it would be better if

I stuck with just the one, he said: 'Sir, how many times a night do you do sex, sir?' I looked at his face from the side. His eyes were glued anxiously on the stony road ahead. He simply wanted to give the best advice that he could. 'It all depends, Babu,' I hedged. 'How about you?' 'Three times, sir,' he said. He was most definite. 'But I do sex with opium, sir. After three times I am sleeping.'

We lapsed into silence. But as we approached our destination, he decided to broach once more the question that had been niggling at his mind ever since he'd first clapped eyes on me standing on the platform with my suitcase. 'Excuse me, sir,' he said. 'Not joke. Are you VIP, sir?'

Again, I hotly denied it. Yet Babu still wasn't convinced either way. And the trivial matter of my importance, or not, must have been troubling him ever since, because this week — two years, roughly, on from that day — he sent an email.

'Hello my dear sir,' it went. 'I asking tourists from England and London about you. They are saying you are famouse and very rich VIP and have palace and many cars. So I am very happy. Have a nice life. Ok by by. babu.'

NO SUGAR STILL
10 May 2014

Sharon's back. As soon as I heard, I went straight round to the house and let myself in. She was standing in the kitchen wearing that deceptively vulnerable look that she has. Also in the room was a little girl aged about three with ruby red hair and a Boxer dog. The Boxer was built like Sonny Liston and capered before me. It span round in circles, glancing coquettishly over its shoulder. The little girl was my superior in intelligence and composure. I could see it straight away, as could she. Her name was Amy. Sharon and her partner had adopted her 18 months before. Sharon and Amy shared a companionable stillness that was unruffled by my appearance.

I hadn't seen Sharon for six months. She was thinner than ever, which made her liquid eyes appear larger. ('It's all gone. She hasn't even got an arse any more,' was how Trev sorrowfully put it when we spoke on the phone later.) She seemed altered in mind as well as body, appearing calmer and kinder and less hunted. This was no longer the Sharon with no limits. I raised Amy by the armpits until her red locks were dangling above me and I reached up and planted a loving kiss on her cheek. She accepted it, looking down at me speculatively. Then I lowered her to the floor and gave Sharon a hug. Thirteen years ago I gave this woman my best shot. It missed. The hug was neutral, formal, slightly tentative.

'Coffee, Jerry?' she said. 'No sugar still?' Then she gave me all her news. Judging by the brio with which she related it, she still lives in 'a tale that is told'. Her mother, her brother, her sister, her poor father: each was a dramatic saga in itself. Then she asked with passionate interest about individual members of my family. I'd never met a person either as wild or as family-minded as Sharon before. Before she came along I'd always imagined the two attitudes were mutually exclusive.

The house sits in a small valley. If you look out of the kitchen window and up, you can see people walking by on the pavement above. Looking past Sharon's blonde head and up at a passer-by, I recognised Tom, another of Sharon's exes. (He was the one after me.) Sharon turned her head just as Tom looked down and recognised her through the kitchen window. He turned and jogged down the slope as though on rails, let himself in through the front door, and here suddenly in the room was Tom.

No one has seen Tom sober for months. He was no different now. Here was the customary red face. Here was the bemused expression on that red face of a man hemmed in by bores and rationalists. Here was the glittering eye and slurred speech. And yet here too were the lightning flashes of total understanding worthy of a savant that one often notices in the permanently pissed.

First Tom sagged in disbelief at finding himself in such august company. Then he turned his attention to the grinning, capering Boxer. He whipped off his sweatshirt and forced its front legs through the arm holes so that the dog was now wearing it. It fitted well. Then he pulled the dog's face to his and snogged it, burying his mouth in the great dribbling Boxer muzzle and kissing with sensuous ardour. Then he spotted the cat, cautiously coming to investigate such an unusual man. Tom then threw away the dog's head and made a great pantomime show of unbuckling his belt and frantically searching in his pants for his locally celebrated penis, as though instantly attracted and changing partners at an orgy.

Then he noticed the little girl standing there eyeing him gravely. He rummaged frantically in his jeans again, in the pocket this time, we were relieved to see. Going down on courtly knee, he presented her with a big square palm with two pennies in it. He was on his way home to bed, he told her. And on the way home he'd stopped at the bookies, and bet £380, which was all the money he possessed, on red, on the roulette machine. He lost. Therefore these pennies represented all he had left in the world. And he would be honoured and proud if she would take one of them. Which would she like? Amy very carefully studied both coins then made her selection. 'What do you say?' said Sharon, kindly. 'Thank you,' said Amy, looking this surprising man candidly in the eye.

Down on one knee still, Tom swivelled to face Sharon. A bolt of white logic had told him the moment he'd walked in that things were different with her now. But just for gallantry and old times' sake, he said, 'And what about you, gorgeous? What about a quick one before I go.'

SHARON IN SARDINIA
10 May 2014

As Sharon stooped to pour boiling water from the kettle into two mugs, I studied her back and wondered what, if anything, remained in me of the love I once had for her. Was there a residue somewhere? Or a stain? I pictured her back as it had been a dozen years earlier, tanned by the Sardinian sun and bisected by the thin turquoise strap of her bikini top.

My love for Sharon was more in the nature of a terrible mental illness than anything nourishing, and when it was at its height, we went away for a week to Santa Teresa Gallura, a quiet seaside town at the northern tip of the island. We stayed in a cool, family-run hotel with views from our window across the blue Strait of Bonifacio to the southern coast of Corsica, and looking the other way, down to the town beach. All week, Sharon wore a pair of bubble-gum pink flip-flops that came free with the latest issue of Cosmopolitan. She also had a new tattoo on that hard back, a blue ascending cherub, and she was obsessed with keeping it moistened with extra daubs of sun cream. On the plane out, I memorised two essential Italian phrases for going abroad with Sharon: lei è vegetarania — she is vegetarian, and puo tenere questi nella cassaforte? — can you keep these in the safe?

At that time Sharon was unhappy with her life and cried all the time. When we'd first met, she'd said to me, 'All I want from you is a good time and an alarm clock.'

Now all she wanted from me was a listening ear while she listed and lamented the causes of her unhappiness, which were more recondite and various than the causes of the first world war.

The town beach was a small, blindingly white cove lapped by a pellucid sea and crowded with Italians. We trooped down there each day with rolled-up towels under our arms. I don't know what sort of Italians they were, or to which Italian social class they belonged, but I felt or imagined we had found ourselves in a society that was both sophisticated and kind. After the first day we seemed to be an instantly recognisable, even popular couple, on that beach, in spite of, or perhaps because of, Sharon's sour face and continual outbreaks of weeping. Nobody stared. But accidentally to catch someone's eye would be instantly rewarded with a beautiful, warm smile, or a friendly 'Ciao!' or even a tanned arm raised in salute.

I remember glancing up for a moment during one of Sharon's jeremiads at five women standing and chatting under a yellow and white striped beach umbrella. Chatting is perhaps too English a word to convey the proximity, the intimacy, the liveliness, the disorderliness, the conviviality, the laughter, the vivacity. Small children clung to some of the legs or played hide-and-seek among them. All the young mums wore surprising sunglasses and arresting swimsuits and were gorgeously tanned, but it was their unaffected delight in each other's company, and in life itself, that stood out. And then I returned my attention reluctantly to this unhappy, tattooed, self-absorbed, orange-fingered, sexually incontinent, bottle-blonde English woman to whom I was horribly enslaved, and refocused my attention on her litany of criticism and complaint.

Why were her hands still trembling so badly when she'd only drunk two bottles of wine last night? Had I not noticed the sarcasm with which that breakfast waitress had said how nice it was to see her down at breakfast this morning? Why had I taken photographs of her that showed her stomach (like Olga Korbut's in her prime) in such a bad light? What was she doing here anyway in this boring place and with someone as boring as me? Why couldn't she find a proper man? Why were all of the men she knew so fundamentally stupid? If she rolled all her current boyfriends into one, they wouldn't make one whole, good man. 'But Sharon,' I gently contended. 'Aren't you confusing intelligence with virtue?'

I remembered how she had snatched up her book — a history of Cosa Nostra — then burst angrily into tears again. I remembered too how, when I got back to England after our holiday, my own rotten infidelity to my girlfriend was discovered three seconds after I returned to her the novel I'd borrowed — with the orange boarding-card stub still in place as a bookmark.

I thought of all these things as I regarded Sharon's back as she made the coffee. Apart from a stab of shame at my former abjectness, I might have been recalling a scene from a half-forgotten film or novel. But that back, though — it was so familiar to me at one time. I like a nice back.

ABOUT THE MERC
12 May 2014

On eBay car auctions one often reads of all sorts of reasons for cars being sold: birth, death, marriage, divorce, promotion, emigration. But rarely is the car an unwanted gift. Terry124 stated that he was selling his Mercedes E320 CDI estate because it was 'a Christmas present for the missis, but she hated it'. After years of scrutinising eBay car ads, I like to think I can distinguish between sellers who have a basic respect for the truth and those who habitually palter with it. But with this one I couldn't decide. It had a ring of truth, certainly, and it ended on a touchingly plaintive note with: 'I'm an honest man.' But the car's description, with the homely bit about 'the missis', could so easily have been an inspired load of flannel designed to appeal to the misogynist community. The car was exactly what I was looking for, however. Low miles, full service history, 'recent new injectors' and standard wheels. So I called the number.

Terry answered. Estuary accent. I told him I wasn't sure I believed the bit about his wife. That was my opener. 'Listen,' he said. 'I'll tell you what happened. My wife likes to go shopping. It's all she does. She's so materialistic, she likes me to pull her knickers down and slap her bottom with my current-account chequebook. We've been married 25 years and I love her to bits. Last Christmas I wanted to get her a car with a bigger boot so she could get more shopping bags in. So after looking at loads of cars for sale,

I bought her an E320 estate. It's got all she wants or needs: a massive boot, vanity mirror light, airbag. The boot's so roomy, her sister's nippers can run around in it. Perfect.

'I thought she'd be so happy with it, she'd be dancing all over the place on the tips of her toes. I thought I'd be allowed to sleep in the house again. But she drove it once and she hated it. She said it was like driving a National Express coach. She hated the car so much she wouldn't even look at it. I told her she'd get used to it. That was it. We had words. We had tears. What's your name again?'

'Jel,' I said.

'Jel, she spilt her popcorn. We had more upset over that car than we've had in the whole of our marriage put together. So I asked her what she wanted instead, and I had to go out and buy her a Skoda. That she likes. She's always had a soft spot for a Skoda. The Merc has been sitting there on the drive ever since. It hasn't been started for three months. I'm looking at it now and it's breaking my heart in two. But she wants it off the drive and out of her life and that's what's going to happen. You know what women are like, Jel.'

'I'm not sure that I do, Terry,' I said.

Terry came across like a man of solid virtue. Or nine tenths virtue, anyway. I said I liked the sound of his Merc, but I'd have to first run his ad past my boy, who is my chief adviser in these matters. My boy said it was a tad overpriced and it was a pity I hadn't gone for the facelift model. Otherwise, he gave me his blessing. Next morning I gave Terry a call. He spoke to me with easy familiarity, as though we'd known each other all our lives. I still wasn't entirely sure whether it was because he had taken a shine to me, or because he was the Izaac Walton of the used-car trade.

He asked me to guess what he did to earn a crust. I guessed lollipop lady. Close, he said. He was a digger driver. 'I sit up here in this earth-mover cab all day long. Sometimes I have ten lorries to load in a day, sometimes a hundred. And you know what, Jel? I'm starting to wonder if there isn't more to life than this. Sometimes I sit up here gnawing at my own vitals with frustration. You should see this site. Massive. A hundred blokes. This morning they told us that from today smoking was banned anywhere on the site and in the cabs. Can you believe it. Four blokes walked there and then. I enjoy a roll-up. I'm smoking one now, as it happens. They can sack me, I don't care. What is the world coming to, Jel, do you reckon, when you can't smoke on a building site?'

'I have no idea, Terry,' I said. 'I can't fathom it out, either. But about the Merc.'

MOTHER SHIP
17 May 2014

I couldn't find the house so I called the number again. Instead of the man I'd spoken to previously, this time a woman answered. 'I'm surprised you couldn't find the house with all your advanced technology,' she said. She sounded elderly. A mid-Devon accent — an older version of it. 'I've yet to join the sat-nav generation, I'm afraid,' I said, apologetically. 'Sat-nav?' she said. 'You must think us very quaint. Stay there and I'll ask Maynard to come and fetch you in his car.'

So I pulled the car over and waited. Five minutes later, a beard driving a Nissan Micra came along, saw me, indicated, slowed down, showed me a palm and performed a U-turn. I started the car and followed him. The careful and helpful way that this man indicated well in advance of each turning, and the excellent condition and cleanliness of his ten-year-old Nissan Micra, and the Christian fish symbol on the back of the car told me in advance that the mower he was selling would be in excellent condition. Even the unobtrusive positioning of the fish was somehow reassuring.

He pulled up outside a tiny cube of pink brick and indicated briskly with an arm that I should park in front of him. I got out and found him already waiting with an outstretched hand. I grasped it and we exchanged comments about the captious weather. He was a spry, intense sort of a man. The beard reminded me of an

Indian fakir's beard. It was groomed, even coiffed. The shaped moustache with its twirly ends was impressive in its own right. But the rest of him — cardigan, collar and tie, diction — was thoroughly British.

He led me around a conifer hedge and there on the postage stamp of the garden was the mower. You could have trimmed a lawn this size with a pair of nail scissors in quarter of an hour, so why he thought he needed a Briggs & Stratton 100 cc engine was anyone's guess. The mower was in showroom condition. He'd even polished the red steel casing. He tilted the machine up on its back wheels and I put my cheek on the ground and peered up at the blades. 'Like new,' I said, getting up. 'I look after my things,' he said, shortly. He bent down and tickled the engine, then pulled the string. The engine fired easily first time. I reached for my cash. But here the stern composure wobbled. Terrified that I might hand over the cash in full view of his prying neighbours, he put an anxious hand on mine and said, 'Let's go indoors.'

He led me through his front door and into a tiny hall that smelt as if it had never been smoked in. Steep carpeted stairs, a gilt hall mirror, and a spindly table with a telephone with a folded copy of the *Daily Mirror* placed on it An elderly woman, presumably the one I'd spoken to earlier, was standing beside this table. She had a very pale face and a scarlet slash of inaccurately applied lipstick. I offered a sunny greeting, but she failed to respond. She seemed to be studying me. I handed the man my four £20 notes. It was a fiver too much and I told him to keep it. He was horrified by that idea, too, and vanished through one of the doors at his back to get change.

The woman and I were now alone together in the claustrophobic hallway. Something about me amused her. 'You're quite convincing, aren't you?' she said. I didn't know how to take this. Perhaps she'd read The Presentation of Self in Every Day Life by Erving Goffman and was referring to my social performance. I thanked her modestly. Then she said, 'You've come a very long way, haven't you?' 'Ten miles. Not far,' I said cheerfully. Her face hardened. 'I'm warning you, I'm not so stupid as the others. I know what you are, and where you have come from, and why. But be aware that we are under God's protection in this house.'

The beard, now returned to the hall brandishing a fiver, was in time to hear this. 'Mavis, please,' he said. Then he gently placed an arm around her and steered her out through the door through which he'd just come. From without I could hear him remonstrating quietly and patiently with her. When he came back, he said, 'She's not quite herself, today.' We shook hands again. 'You know your way back from here, do you?' he said. 'To the mother ship?' I said. The pink slit in the beard widened. Beneath all that hair, I now noticed, was a kind, humorous face. 'Turn left at the bottom, then left again, then just keep going till you know where you are,' he said.

SECONDS OUT
19 May 2014

In the blue corner, wearing 4oz gloves, is the Ninja. Real name Klynton. The younger of my two grandsons. Also known as Ninge. Aged three. Weighed in at 35lbs. Blue eyes, blond hair. Not yet fluent in the language. Has only one word — juvvy. Nobody knows what juvvy is. Possibly a neologism. The word is now in common and versatile use within the family as a substitute for any noun. Example: 'What's on the juvvy tonight?' Otherwise as mute as a fish. We've tried him in French and drawn a blank there also. Once a week his father takes him to Chatter Time, a pre-school group for three-year-olds.

The Ninja appears preoccupied by a private world that is even more interesting than this one. He is impervious to physical pain. He is only aware of mental pain. Easily irritated. Hair-trigger temper. Becomes enraged at the intransigence of inanimate objects. Cries pitifully if he loses sight of his father, even when his father is in the same room. Otherwise a radiant, slightly blank smile. Favourite pastime: opening and shutting things. His passion in life. Unless forcibly prevented, he will open and shut a door, or a drawer, or a kitchen cupboard door with unflagging interest for hours. Loves his grub. Eats anything. Loves his bed. Looks forward every night to going there. Settles down into it with an expression on his face of ineffable joy, just like his grandfather. His visiting care worker says there is nothing wrong with him. Says that some children begin to speak much later than others. Says it might be a confidence thing. Says that if it turns out that the Ninja is on the autism spectrum, she doesn't know anything about children. We think he is, and that she doesn't. But we don't care. He's a fine chap. His fighting stance is unorthodox. He is holding his gloves way out in front like a sleepwalker and he is rolling his head in ecstasy. The big money bets are on him to win in the first round. But that stance and attitude has his backers exchanging anxious looks.

In the red corner, also in the 4oz gloves for the first time — Mr Chops. Real name Oscar. The elder grandson. Aged four and a half. Weighed in at 37lbs. Blue eyes, blond hair. Fluent in the language. Too fluent, if you ask his father. A confident, non-stop speaker. Says words like finally, unfortunately and Madagascar. Writes his name with an 'a' for apple that looks too much like a 'q' for queen but thinks he has cracked the writing game. Knows where Madagascar is on an atlas. Knows everything already, in fact. Furiously angry if gainsaid. Vivid imagination. Less keen on being kissed and hugged than he was when he was young. Can pass his finger slowly through a candle flame and back again.

Punches himself in the head and falls down when bored. His laugh currently a work in progress. Throws back his head and laughs like a pantomime villain. It's that or nothing. Alarming. Enjoys driving. Beats his grandfather at dominoes and memory card games. Cheats deplorably without guile or compunction. Hates losing. Absolutely refuses. Interested in colours. Can jump from the fifth stair. Likes to play football in the garden with his shirt off. Any excuse to take his shirt off. Kicks the ball like a pro with the outside of his foot. Can do headers. Favourite book at the moment: *The Day Louis Got Eaten*. Health generally good. Willy currently blackened by impetigo, but responding well to treatment. Attends pre-school class four days a week. Has two best friends, Tom and Jack, neither of whom will consent to play with him. It is the one great sadness of his life. Mr Chops favoured punch is the uncontrolled haymaker, delivered like a discus. His fighting stance is the double arm windmill action.

I am about to tinkle my little bell for the start of round one when their father appears. It has been a difficult year for their father. He is raising the boys singlehandedly and working 12-hour shifts in a nursing home. He is wan and permanently exhausted. Despairing looks are the only ones I get from him these days. He comes in looking crazy, his pale-blue carer's smock under his jacket, and sinks down into a chair. The young amateur boxers dash over to their father — their favourite punchbag — climb up on to his chair, and administer a damn good leathering. Their father cowers weakly in his chair as the blows rain down. 'Good day at the office?' I ask him. He looks out at me between the blows and I get another one of those desperate looks.

DAYMER BAY
24 May 2014

Just when I was beginning to think I'd had enough, I was offered a free week in a caravan. I took it like a shot, threw a few shirts in the boot of the car, and buggered off down to Cornwall. I arrived in darkness and couldn't find the electricity switch. But I was so tired I simply climbed into a sleeping bag by the light of my phone and fell asleep.

I was woken by sunshine and the cawing of rooks. At this caravan, there is no internet, no phone signal for miles, no telly, no radio. And the air I swear is soporific. It was like crawling out of my sleeping bag on a different, quieter planet. But being out of my usual element, and released, suddenly, from the continual demands of other people, and their noise, and their terrifying, overpowering wills, and then breathing the different, softer Cornish air, had a peculiar effect on me. With the pressure suddenly off, I sort of caved in, and found I'd lost both manual dexterity and the ability to think logically or consecutively. I couldn't do up the sleeping-bag zip, not even after puzzling and teasing at it for half an hour. I couldn't do up my shirt buttons. I put them in the wrong holes. I fluffed tying the laces of my shoes. I couldn't slop apple juice into a mug without spillage. Folding back the many curtains and fastening them in the fiddly curtain ties seemed an almost insuperable operation.

Even in broad daylight I couldn't locate the caravan's electricity master switch. I all but dismantled the propane gas boiler in an effort to make it go and have hot water running through the shower head — and I still failed. I couldn't get the little bluetooth music speaker I'd bought for exactly this kind of situation to work at any price. I couldn't open a packet of biscuits with either my fingers or my teeth. I tried with a blunt knife and failed. I couldn't find a sharp knife. The cawing of the rooks began to sound threatening and unpleasant. I caught sight of myself — a staring maniac — in the mirror above the decorative mantelpiece. I slumped down on to a bench and noticed that my joints ached and I had the beginnings of a headache. I wanted to smash something, anything, and not excluding myself.

I retied and fastened my shoelaces, agonised for perhaps five minutes about whether or not to take my coat, looked everywhere in a furious rage for the caravan's door key and found it in my pocket, then I quit the caravan, slamming the door behind me with all of my little strength. At the gate I could choose to turn right on to a track of stark white dust, or I could turn left. The choice seemed to be somehow crucially important and I was paralysed by that. Fearing the worst, I turned left. Twenty yards along I changed my mind and walked back the other way. I came to the entrance to the beach and some surfwear shops and their fluttering flags. I turned left, went up the hill and turned right on to the coastal footpath. The path led across a rabbit-cropped lawn and suddenly I was out and away with a glittering ocean on my right, a cloudless blue heaven above, and pink sea campion bobbing and nodding agreement all around me. An elderly couple, brimming with vitality and goodwill, greeted me with utmost cordiality as they sped past in the opposite direction. I returned their greeting like a game-show host yelling end-of-show inanities above the roar of an applauding audience. Now, I realised, I was as crazily elated above reasonableness as I had been earlier depressed below it.

After a mile I arrived at the mouth of the Camel river and behind it the sandy expanse of Daymer bay, which looks exactly like the river Niger as it runs through the Sahel near Mopti in Mali. I was flying. I took off my shoes and socks and stalked barefoot right across the bay, sometimes on the scalding sand, sometimes at the water's edge, sometimes paddling through it. A school of porpoises, half a dozen of them, bloody great things, like whales seen from a distance, were sporting or browsing in the estuary not 50 yards away, and I kept my neck craned and my eye on them constantly as I walked. The sunlight glancing off sea and sand was dazzling. Sweat stung my eyes. The air shimmered above the sandy wastes and what seemed close at hand turned out to be far away and vice versa. But I kept my eye on my friends the porpoises, envying their shiny blackness, and their effortless wheeling, which reminded me of something I'd recently lost, but also lent confidence that I might recover it soon enough.

HIS MAJESTY, THE BABY
31 May 2014

I was two days alone in the caravan and no signal or reception of any sort. It was like a Buddhist silent retreat, where you have to listen in horrified amazement to your own thoughts. During the day I walked the cliff path; in the evenings I sat on the caravan steps wishing I had a rook rifle. On my walks, I did acquire a book, however: Sigmund Freud's essay On Narcissism. It was on a community book-swap shelf in a disused telephone box. I've been picking up Freud and putting him down again perplexed and defeated for most of my adult life. But when I opened this one and glanced inside, I thought here at last was something I might be able to get to grips with.

A narcissist, I read, standing outside the peeling kiosk, is 'someone who treats his own body in the same way in which the body of a sexual object is ordinarily treated — who looks at it, that is to say, strokes it and fondles it until he obtains complete satisfaction through these activities'. Well, blow me down, old Sigmund had me down to a tee, the fella. So that's what I am — a narcissist. I couldn't wait to get the book back to the caravan, draw the curtains, and settle down to read in a calm and leisurely manner what is going on behind the scenes.

I started off well. I could understand successive sentences. Early in his career, says Freud, he had all us narcissists down as perverts. Then over time, he says, he kindly modified that view and now concedes that this kind of human behaviour is perhaps fairly normal. Pleased about that, but wondering about such a sheltered life as his must have been, I pressed on. But soon the road ran out and I was blundering hopelessly about in a dense and thorny thicket of object-cathexes, ego-instincts and transference neuroses. Before I flung the book aside, however, I stumbled, scratched and bleeding, into a clearing. Children, Freud says, are pure narcissists. That is why we imagine we love them. Their blithe narcissism revives and speaks to the narcissist in us that we as socially adjusted adults have been forced to repress. 'Parental love,' he concludes, 'which is so moving and at bottom so childish, is nothing but the parents' narcissism born again.'

What a bastard, I thought. He's drawn the rug out from under our feet. But like an infection his idea took insidious hold in spite of my sergeant-majorly contempt for it. During my walks I saw dotard parents propelling their little ones about in their elaborate pushchair equivalents of the royal carriage, and deferring to them as though they were little emperors and empresses — or 'His Majesty the baby' as Freud puts it. Then my son drove down, deposited his four-and-a-half-year-old son with me, and drove away again. And for three days and nights my grandson and I — in Freudian terms two 'primary' narcissists — lived together in a static caravan.

Since his birth I have been entirely besotted with my grandson. It's become a family joke. 'How's Oscar?' they say to me, just to see my eyes light up with folly. It's that innocently put cattle-prod question. I have often wondered how and why such a powerful feeling has come over me completely out of the blue. 'Why did nobody warn me?' I say in mock complaint.

And in four and a half years, we've never had a cross word.

But during those three days we had nothing but cross words. We were a pair of warring narcissists cooped up together in a three-bedroom Festival Super, because my grandson has recently added to his narcissism an ugly megalomania. He now wants to set the pace, decide the itinerary, and interpret the world for me. 'Look, an aeroplane!' he said, pointing to a giant wind turbine on a hillside. 'That's not an aeroplane, it's a windmill.' 'It's an aeroplane.' 'No, it's a windmill. If it's an aeroplane, why isn't it moving?' 'It's an aeroplane.' And then a furious, pouting sulk. He could not be wrong on any subject. He was omnipotent and omniscient. He was indeed acting exactly like a Tudor monarch. But I was an argumentative courtier. The narcissist in me flatly refused to bow the knee. I argued the toss with him, I harangued him, I threatened to depose him. He put his fingers in his ears and smiled regally at me. But something changed between us in those three days. I think my defiant challenge to his divine authority has yet to be forgiven, and I'm no longer his court favourite. And now, thankfully, we can move on.

COMEBACK
14 June 2014

My first time back in the local for eight weeks. The manageress lifts the flap, comes around to my side of the bar and kisses me on the lips. We can't hear ourselves speak as there is a ska DJ barricaded into a corner behind a waist-high wall of speakers and the bar is small and the ceiling low. She indicates that my gin and tonic is on the house. I take it outside and take a seat on one of the picnic benches on the patio. This hippie guy is prancing ecstatically around the tables with fluttering fingers.

A couple sit themselves down opposite me and the bloke starts rolling a single skin joint. I know them by sight but I don't know either of their names. While he concentrates his energies on rolling the spliff, the woman reassures me with great earnestness and intensity that I look fantastic. You know how some people have that hollowed-out, cadaverous look, she says? I should take it from her that I do not have this look.

Then Trev arrives. He's wearing his customary conservative cream shirt with collar. Most uncharacteristically, however, he's puffing on one of those vaporiser cigarettes. I never thought I'd see the day. He puffs on it continuously, like a pipe. Blackcurrant and banana flavour, he says. I'm looking good, he says — for a mutant.

It's only a tiny spliff, but when the bloke sparks it up, smoke pours from the end like a bonfire of wet leaves. And the smell is unbelievably pungent. We're all flapping our hands disgustedly in front of our noses. He offers it to Trev. Trev sanctimoniously tells him he's given up smoking. He offers it to me. I take a small puff on it just to be sociable and hand it back. Twenty seconds later, I find that psychologically speaking I'm terribly altered. And then the barman comes out and says, lads, lads, please, no weed, please, we can all smell it in the bar. The bloke who rolled it promptly hands it to me. I hand it to Trev. Trev offers it to the barman. The barman shakes his head and retreats back inside.

A minute later the other bar server, a woman, comes flying out. She's disgusted and furious, she says, because she's losing customers because of the smell. We're all well into our fifties and we sit there smirking and denying everything like guilty children. It wasn't us, says Trev, pointing to a table of clean-cut teens, it was them over there. She looks at the happily chatting youngsters, looks at us, goes to say something, thinks better of it and turns on her heel. All this has occurred between the first and the second sip of my drink.

Trev and I pick up our drinks and go inside. I notice that he is staying solicitously close, as if I am in a fragile condition. I am indeed feeling slightly tired this evening and uncharacteristically we sit down and listen to the music and watch the dancers, who are mostly women. Trev seems to know an awful lot about every single one of them. He sits beside me like a bloodstock agent pointing out this one and then that one and assessing their relative merits. Forget that one over there, he says. The figure might be out of this world, but she hates men. Now, see that one over there? She might not look that much, but underneath all that crap she's wearing is one tidy body. And she's a nice maid, too. A lovely little maid, actually. She'd do me, he says. I notice that he and I have tiny points of blue and yellow light playing and dancing all over us and our drinks. The DJ comes out from behind his speaker barricade and shakes my hand warmly. I've forgotten his name as well. He's the singer in a fantastic local ska band called the Simmertones. He humbly presents me with a signed copy of their latest CD. This is all beginning to feel uncomfortably elegiac.

I confide to Trev that I'm feeling a little tired and perhaps I ought to go home. Trev changes his manner from that of a bloodstock agent to that of a doctor. Now look here, he says. What you need are a few Jägerbombs. They'll sort you out. So obediently I go to the bar and order ten. The barman knocks two quid off — an unheard of thing. We drink some and give some away and Trev's quite right: I now feel quite different again and the tiredness has vanished. I look at the pub clock, thinking it must be nearly closing time. I'm astonished to see I've been in the pub for just three quarters of an hour. I take my jacket off, carefully fold it, and stow it under our seat.

SHARON GOES TO PAMPLONA
17 June 2014

Then there was the time I took Sharon to the Pamplona bull run. She looked very fetching in the traditional St Fermín costume of white T-shirt, white cut-off jeans, red sash tied around the waist and the red neckerchief symbolising the saint's martyrdom by beheading. She wore her neckerchief in a big rumpled V at the front, like a cowgirl.

The Sanfermines last a week. Hundreds of thousands of young revellers cram into the old fortress town's narrow streets and cane it. As well as the famous bull runs each morning, and the evening bullfights, there are fairs and parades and marching bands and pop concerts and a nightly firework display competition that is worth going for on its own. One year the Basque separatists exploded a bomb in a side street during the festivities and no one noticed. There is a special nude running of the bulls, without bulls, by animal rights protesters, and one for the kiddies one year with the bulls represented by a man with horns on his head. But excessive drinking is the main thing.

We arrived on the first day and parked the car in the grounds of a monastery, about half a mile from the town. We walked down to the town and joined the fray. At the first bar we stopped at, the barman, referring to Sharon with a tilt of his head, said to me: 'Novia?' Novia in Spanish means sweetheart or betrothed. It is pronounced 'nobia'. I looked at Sharon standing there at the bar looking beautiful, angry and stoned. Then I shook my head sadly. 'No nobia,' I said.

Soon after that I lost her in the crowd and I didn't see her again for three days. But at Pamplona the people you go with are rarely the people you see most of. Then I bumped into her unexpectedly in the town square. Unlike my own and most other people's, her white T-shirt and jeans were still snow-white and miraculously uncreased. This puzzled me, until it occurred to me that she probably hadn't been wearing them much. She was alone and striding out purposefully. I thought she was going to ignore me, but she took my hand and asked me if I'd like to take some amphetamine sulphate with her. I said it would be a pleasant reminder of my golden adolescence and we repaired to one of the many bars on the square's perimeter.

The narrow bar was packed to the rafters and in an uproar. I recognised the place as the bar where the famous Brooklyn bull runner Joe Distler was reputed to hang out. Up to now I'd avoided the place, as I'd imagined it to be full of pious, bickering, English-speaking taurine intellectuals. Not so. A sort of hellish pandemonium reigned. As Sharon kissed and hugged and high-fived her way through the sweaty, raucous crowd to the toilet at the back, I saw that she had taken to the madness of Pamplona like a duck to water.

The single-cubicle toilet was down a narrow flight of stairs. We squeezed in and I closed and bolted the door behind us. Sharon emptied the wrap on the cistern top and chopped adeptly at the powder with the edge of her Boots Advantage card. Someone began hammering persistently on the door. The fist was joined by one then several others. The hammering became a continuous thunder. Boots were added to the fists, then shoulders. A serious and concerted effort was being made to smash the door in.

We were in a race against time, it appeared. I braced my hands against the back wall and my backside against the door to form a buttress. But Sharon was in no hurry. The drama of the situation seemed only to relax her. She bent calmly and gracefully to her line, took it up her nose, then stood and inhaled deeply through her nostrils as though she were taking in the invigorating air on top of Beachy Head. The door by now was coming off its hinges, the thunder of the kicking deafening. Goodness knows how many people were out there, or what was the general point they were making.

Sharon tilted the rolled-up banknote in those long slender fingers of hers and angled it towards me. I looked into her eyes. The door was now right off its hinges and the shouting became a confused roaring. As those huge clouded eyes regarded mine, I saw that they were entirely serene. She was in her element. It was the calmest, profoundest moment of our relationship. It was worth going just for that. Holding her gaze, I unhurriedly slid the note from between her fingers and bent to the cistern top as the door and goodness knows how many people fell in on top of us.

AFTER SCHOOL
27 June 2014

Oscar!' cried Miss Herd as I arrived. She was standing at the classroom door releasing her charges one by one as the parent, or in my case the grandparent, arrived to escort them safely back to their respective homes. Oscar came solemnly out in his navy Academy sweatshirt carrying his red Fireman Sam lunchbox and placed his four-year-old hand in his grandfather's 57-year-old one. We headed off to the car. 'Did Tom play with you today?' I said. Tom, by all reports, is omnipotent and capricious in his choice of playmates. 'No,' said Oscar tragically.

I was standing in on the school run for Daddy, who had to work an extra 12-hour shift at the care home unexpectedly. Oscar lives with Daddy and goes to stay with Mummy at the weekends. 'Are you having me?' said Oscar. 'Until eight o'clock,' I said. 'Is that long?' he said. 'Very,' I said. He looked up, pleased.

Before we did anything else, grandad had to go to the doctor's for a depot anti-testosterone injection in the bum. While we were inthe waiting area he sat on my lap and I read him a picture story called Rupert and the Pirates. Rupert was kidnapped by three vicious-looking, ill-mannered pirates, and one much older pirate with a kind face who eventually helped Rupert to escape. We wondered why such a decent old man should be keeping such disreputable company in the first place. When Rupert returned with a burly, laid-back policeman, the pirate with a kind face grassed up his mates, and the copper took his good behaviour into account and let him off with a caution.

And on that happy note we went into the treatment room, where Oscar sat on a chair clutching his red plastic lunchbox and watched as the practice nurse punctured grandad in the buttock of his choice with a syringe. The nurse was extra cheerful, even festive, with a small witness present, and afterwards presented him with a Biro sponsored by a drug company as a souvenir. Then he put his small hand in mine again and we went out. 'I like your shirt,' he said when we were out in the street again.

After that we went to a literary festival. The main event was being held in a medieval banqueting hall. We sat on deckchairs on the lawned courtyard outside, eating peppermint ice cream from tubs with plastic scoops located in the lids, while observing the festival-goers coming and going. They were all fearfully old and not noticeably festive, though from time to time the current speaker in the Great Hall must have made a jest, because a gale of elderly, relieved, literary-minded laughter, amplified in the vast space between them and the hammer-beam roof, seeped out through the stained-glass windows.

We played a game of picking out individual festival-goers and guessing how old they were. 'How old do you think he is?' I said, pointing out a gentleman of about 90, gamely feeling his way along the path with two sticks. 'Twenty?' said Oscar. Then we went to the secondhand bookshop, where Oscar only partially succeeded in concealing his boredom. I bought for myself a biography of Frank Weston, Bishop of Zanzibar from 1907–24; and for Oscar and myself equally, The Tale of Pigling Bland.

'I was patient, wasn't I?' said Oscar, inserting his hand in mine again as we went out. His use of a word describing such an abstract concept surprised me, and together we dissected its meaning in case he thought it meant merely that he had been bored out of his skull.

Then we went to the leisure centre learner pool, where Oscar made his Great Leap Forward. The week before he had bravely submerged his head beneath the surface for the first time. Today, while his submerged grandad sat smiling encouragement and giving him the thumbs up, Oscar found the courage not only to submerge his entire self, but also to take his feet off the tiles and propel himself forwards three yards under the water. We celebrated afterwards with onion rings and Slush Puppies all round, large blue ones, in the leisure centre café.

Then we went home and read *The Tale of Pigling Bland*, in which another burly policeman calmly arrests a pig whose papers aren't in order. Then we ate crisp-bottomed fried eggs on toast, and at ten past eight, Daddy, pale with exhaustion, appeared in the doorway wearing his sky-blue care assistant's shift. 'So what have you been up to, Oscar?' he said. Oscar cocked his head and thought about it. 'Can't remember,' he confessed. 'Well, you can have ten more minutes, then it's bedtime.' 'Is that long?' said Oscar. I thought about explaining how time is ultimately relative then thought better of it. 'No, not very,' I said.

SPECTATOR PARTY TIME
19 July 2014

They do love a party at *The Spectator*. I was invited to four in ten days last week: the Apollo Summer party, the *Spectator* 'At Home' Summer party, the annual *Spectator* 'Meet the Readers' afternoon tea party, and our *Spectator* arts editor, the great Liz Anderson's farewell party.

I hadn't been up to town this year, and on the train journey up from Devon, I felt like a hick up from the sticks. But I love London and I had that same old heart-lift as I stepped down from the train under the great iron roof of Paddington station, then passed along the platform beneath that giant unkempt simpleton representing the Great Western Railway employees who fell in the first world war. But my favourite arriving-in-London moment was yet to come.

I went six stops on the Bakerloo line, climbed up out of Charing Cross station into the dazzle and wingbeat of Trafalgar Square's airy 50 acres. Then I crossed the road, passed under Admiralty Arch, glimpsed a sunlit Buckingham Palace at the end of the Mall, and turned sharp left at that sinister old second world war concrete bunker, from which presumably Churchill would have made his last stand if it had come to it.

On my right now was glorious St James's Park, with its surprising pelicans and that quaint old park keeper's cottage, and the public conveniences hidden by shrubbery, which is also a cottage, in that very modern sense of the word, and a very lively one. The foreign tourists who pass in and out of there must marvel at the number of attendants standing about with apparently nothing to do, and perhaps regard this as a manifestation of a high civilisation. Then, on my left, coming into view now, was the magnificent open space of Horseguards Parade, formerly a tiltyard, adorned by the pugnacious Old Admiralty Building, with George Gilbert Scott's Italianate Foreign Office beyond. From here I could see Birdcage Walk, with a glimpse, through the trees, of the Spectator office garden — my destination.

I was wearing my suit, a new shirt ripped from the cellophane, and a pink tie. A pentecostal London wind was blowing the tie straight out in front of me, where it hovered as if by magic. My shoes were polished, my hair newly cut, and I'd shaved that morning with a new razor blade. Big Ben chimed musically, then came that hair-raising hiatus before the terrible certainty of that first stroke. In about another three minutes, I will be walking in through the light oak door of 22 Old Queen Street and giving my name at the reception desk.

It is always here, at this precise moment, as I'm walking across Horseguards Parade, that I feel I have arrived in London. I'm sober, clean, dressed in all my finery, and back in our great capital after an absence in the country. Furthermore, I am going to a Spectator party, which are the best kind of parties I know of. I am confident that everyone I meet there will be cheerful, friendly, courteous, funny, intelligent, well-dressed, not judgmental, and as serious or as lighthearted as you like. But above all you can have a drink. There is never any shortage. It's ridiculous. If I haven't been up to town for a while, hick-like I tend to cane it, often with unfortunate results. And I know through long and painful experience that right at this moment, conscious of Horseguards' fine gravel through the thin soles of my dancing shoes, I am feeling the best physically that I am going to feel for a while.

I continued along Horseguards as far as Birdcage Walk, crossed over into Storey's Gate, turned right into Old Queen Street, and went in through the door of number 22, giving my name at the desk. I went along the passage, down the stairs, picked up a flute of champagne from the table in the music room and passed through into the garden. The first person I saw was Michael Heath, who, as soon as he saw me, cried, 'Oh no!' — or words to that effect — and threw up his arms in horror. And so we began. The last person I spoke to, at the final party, Liz Anderson's farewell, was Boris. He was standing alone on the garden steps. I haven't seen him standing alone anywhere since he edited the paper. He had a short, sharp haircut and was wearing an electric-blue suit. I was drunk. He offered his paw. 'Nice suit,' I observed. 'I had it made in China,' he said, opening the jacket wide to show me how capacious it was. 'I'm in the Chinese tent,' he added, making an up-to-date political joke even of his suit. And then I went to Paddington, and from there back to Devon to lick my wounds, and try to remember as much of it as I could.

WHY DIDN'T YOU STOP?
9 September 2014

I've might have no testosterone. (My production is currently being stopped by injection once every three months.) But what I do have is a Fiat Barchetta, bought for a grand on a whim on eBay. It's the prettiest little two-seater, an old-school, fun drive, with a lot of growl and it makes people smile. Left-hand drive. I've had it a month and so far I have yet to see another on the road.

The one obvious change thus far in my testosterone-free personality is my taste in music. I've gone from liking aggressive stuff like ZZ Top and AC/DC to preferring soppy Nick Drake and Joni Mitchell. The theme from Out of Africa. Gentler stuff. Triteness. I love you-oo. Also tabernacle choirs. Even folk. So I was belting along in my Barchetta under a windswept sky, Fairport Convention barely audible over the rumble of the exhaust, the road ahead long and straight, the moorland on either side wantonly disfigured by wind turbines.

My position on wind turbines (for what it is worth) is that I enjoy looking at the big ones. Those that are so enormous they beggar belief have a kind of majesty, I think. Or maybe that's the lack of testosterone speaking. But these ones were elderly, small and crowded, and one was conscious only of a cretinous contempt for the landscape.

At intervals the road passed through straggling villages, narrowing as it did so. Parked cars on either side of the road in these villages constricted the way still further. I was sailing through one such village, disturbing the peace, when I clipped the wing mirror of a parked car, knocking out my own mirror. There was nowhere to stop in the village, not even a bus stop, and seconds later I was out the other side, on fast, open road again. Here, of course, if I were a gentleman, I should have stopped the car, turned around and returned to the scene to assess any damage. And I did feel a slight prick to what's left of my conscience. But the clear road ahead invited me to press the toe down and forget all about it. Which, I am ashamed to say, is precisely what I did.

Then I noticed that my mirror, though fallen out, was dangling freely. I swerved sharply into a convenient lay-by screened from the road by trees, got out, and tried without success to clip the mirror back in. I was persevering in this, when a five-year-old Ford Focus with two people in it came screeching up. It took several seconds to realise that this was the car I'd knocked. They must have been sitting in it at the time, and had come haring up the road after me.

A man of about 45 got out, but stayed close to his car. He was trembling with anger, or perhaps the excitement of the chase, or both. His physique suggested that he had spent his life in a sedentary occupation, for which I gave thanks. His passenger, a woman, stayed put.

'Why didn't you stop?' he asked entirely reasonably. I walked over to take a look at his nearside wing mirror, expecting nothing much. He looked the type to make a fuss about nothing. It would be cracked or missing mirror at worst, I guessed. But on the contrary, his wing mirror and casing were totally wrecked. The mirror, electrics, indicator pane, bulb, casing were all smashed. I couldn't have been more surprised. I bent down to examine the wreckage out of morbid interest as much as anything else.

The woman in the passenger seat had a hard, 40-a-day face. 'Why didn't you stop?' she said to me through the open window. The correct and truthful answer was because whatever the damage I'd done, I thought I would get away with it. 'I didn't think I'd done any damage to yours,' I said, doing my bit for the nation's moral decline. 'Certainly not that much.' She looked away out of the passenger side window in disgust and refused to look at me again.

The bloke seemed a decent sort. He was angry, but also devastated, as if it was one of the most terrible things that had happened to him. Seeing that, I was penitent. 'How much to fix it?' I said. He said his brother-in-law owned the same make and model, and the same thing happened to him, and the bill was £175. I had £200 in my pocket, fished it out and offered it to him, with a sincere apology. The woman still had her gaze averted. 'You should have stopped,' she said. Accepting the folded cash, the man said, 'Accidents happen, I suppose.' It was gallant of him to say it, but the stock phrase caught in his throat. And he was still trembling with anger.

NORTH DEVON GAZETTE
16 September 2014

I live in south Devon. Last week I went up to north Devon, to visit a friend who was renting a cottage on the coast for a week. Devon is a big county. I decided to go by train to Barnstaple and then by bus. At Exeter the train caught fire, however, and we were herded off and packed into an old charabanc that could barely get up the steep Exmoor hills.

At Barnstaple, finally, I waited at stand J of the austere bus station. Punctually, a minibus drew up and six of us climbed on: a blond lad with airline tags on his backpack; a man-mountain in a baggy suit carrying a guitar case; a middle-class woman who greeted the driver with genial condescension; a pair of teenage lovers, she showing as much as possible of an exciting pair of thighs; and me. The driver had long hair and looked like an old biker. There was something irredeemably unofficial about him, as though he'd stolen the bus for a laugh after a drinking session. 'Oh look, a millionaire!' he exclaimed as I riffled through my wad looking for something smaller than a 20.

The hour-long journey cost three quid. I sat at the back and read a discarded *North Devon Gazette*. The only reported crime that week was an all-girl brawl on Minehead seafront. One sustained bruising to her head. Soon we were barrelling across a high hogsback road with rich, rolling farmland on either side. A gale blew violently through the bus, buffeting our hair this way and that, and

I totally lost control of the *North Devon Gazette*. The driver threw the bus around in a swashbuckling, exhilarating manner while shouting a conversation against the wind and the engine roar with the middle-class woman. The young sweethearts sitting in front of me were drunk on youth or alcohol or love or all three. They had eyes only for each other. Hers shone with adoration. For them I didn't even exist. And rightly so. For mile after noisy, lurching mile they fenced furiously with empty plastic Highland Spring bottles. At one point they lowered their weapons and he leaned forward and put his lips softly against her forehead. She accepted his blessing with the peace and reverence of a supplicant at the communion rail.

Stopping outside a village newsagent, the driver came out from behind his wheel and announced that he was going in to buy lottery tickets. A splendid idea. Everybody rose — everybody except the teenage lovers, who already possessed in their youth and in each other riches far exceeding any lottery win — and followed the driver off the bus and into the newsagent's. I was beginning to like our driver and his swashbuckling ways. He was genuinely and unselfconsciously a man of the people. Any power, authority or glamour that his position as bus driver might have earned him in these far-flung communities was violently repudiated by a piratical demeanour. He roughly hailed and was hailed in return by everyone in the shop. Even the style with which he bought lottery tickets brought to mind a gambling-mad Long John Silver who has had himself rowed secretly ashore for the purpose.

I bought a single lucky dip. It seems to me now that there is more chance of being murdered in your bed in a case of mistaken identity than of coming up with three, let alone six, numbers. I handed over my coins without a shred of hope. We climbed back aboard the bus united and exalted by our unscheduled gambling stop. I asked the young backpacker if he'd come far. Yes, from Tanzania, he said. The driver threw himself back into his driving seat and slammed his little stable door behind him with a detonation that startled even the teenage lovers.

In the next valley the bus was flagged down by a desperado. After a hasty negotiation with the driver, he was allowed to stand on the step and ride shotgun. A little way up the road we came upon a runaway child. The man jumped down and then jumped back up again as the child spotted him and sprinted away. The driver drove slowly after the boy, and was touchingly careful not to run him down. Everyone on the bus except the teenage lovers craned forward as the drama unfolded. Suddenly, in an inspired move, the escapee doubled back, and the man leapt off the moving bus and we watched the continued pursuit through the back window until they were out of sight.

The driver slammed the bus up through the gears and soon we were bowling along with the wind blowing through the bus again as though we were flying. I took up the *North Devon Gazette* again, folded it in half three times, and settled down to read about a boy who'd got a nail in his foot while playing on a seesaw.

SCORING MUD
27 September 2014

Stand outside the fishmongers in 20 minutes and call this number,' she said, 'and I can arrange it.' On Saturday evening I was scrubbed up for a big night out. I was wearing a black jacket and black jeans, which is overdressed for a night out in this seaside town. But Jupiter, said Shelley von Strunckel, was making a spectacular conjunction with Uranus, my ruler, lending me enormous powers of attraction. So I thought I might as well dress up for the occasion. After 20 minutes, I stood outside the fishmongers and called the number. Half a minute later an anonymous-looking door next to the shop opened inwards, and she waved me inside and led the way up a flight of uncarpeted stairs and into a small, brightly lit kitchen with two good-looking women in it, both wreathed in welcoming smiles. My arranger introduced me with some pride as 'a writer'. I couldn't let this go by without a correction, which was that I was 'a sort of journalist'. But even that seemed to impress and inspire them. I strongly fancied the both of them. One had on a strappy number revealing a caramel tan and a tattoo of South America, including rivers. 'Would you like to go upstairs?' she said. 'Righty-ho,' I said, and I followed them up.

The stairs led to a large room in which a dozen or so young people were lounging on mattresses and cushions. Hats are back, I was glad to see. I was obliged to step carefully into the room to avoid knocking over some formidable-looking bongs, which were dotted about like plastic gnomes at a garden centre. I also nearly stepped on a cardboard box stacked with little dove-grey canisters of (presumably) nitrous oxide. Joints were being constructed. An air of relaxation, irenic affability and timelessness prevailed. Again I was introduced to the company erroneously as a 'writer'. 'Dude,' they said. 'Don't get up,' I said. 'He looks more like a banker,' observed a beanie hat delicately sticking three cigarette papers together.

I was asked where I lived. I gave the name of a village some 20 miles away, which provoked a mild, irrelevant and absurdly prolonged argument about its exact location, as if they were a debating society glad of a subject at last. 'We all went out last night and none of us has been to bed yet,' explained Miss South America. 'Would you like a drink?'

It was nine o'clock in the evening. For someone who had been awake for nearly two days, she looked as fresh as a daisy, though a little distant perhaps. But even from a distance she was friendly and inviting. 'What have you got?' I said, slightly surprised that alcohol was also available. She picked her way slowly and gracefully across the room to see what they had left, raising her arms like a tightrope walker at tricky points. After a long minute of study and contemplation of some bottles, and much indecision, she finally returned with a tall glass containing, she said apologetically, rum and ginger beer, which I knocked back thirstily in one, being a little hard of hearing these days, and not having heard the 'rum' part of the description.

I had intended to make my purchase as quickly as possible and return to my circle of sad old gits gathered in a pub down the road. Now, I decided, I much preferred the company of this laidback gang of twenty-something-year-olds, who, in spite of working their way through a pharmacy over two days, were maintaining a spirit of kindness, openness and congeniality, even to an elderly man dressed as their idea of a banker. If this is a rising generation of drug-addled wasters and reprobates, I like it very much. Plus there was Miss South America, still on her feet and delightfully playing the hostess.

But now I was introduced to the retailer-in-chief, a hatless and polite young guy who looked as though he hadn't eaten for a month. He'd run out of bags, he said, patting his pockets distractedly. He had to go back to his flat for more anyway, he said, so why didn't I come along, which was very trusting of him. So I embraced Miss South America goodbye and answered some valedictory raised fists with one of my own. Then I embraced Miss South America once more, and kissed her earlobe, and off we went to his place.

But it was all a waste of time as things turned out. Owing perhaps to the magnetic influence of Jupiter, I drank far too much that night and had to lie face down on the comfortable pavement outside the last club we went to; whereupon, I can only conclude, some shrinking violet must have relieved me of the contents of my pockets, my purchase included.

MR WHAT'S-THE-TIME?
28 September 2014

I woke up in the foetal position, on my back, on Trev's tiny sofa, with an old curtain over me. This curtain was a step up from the tea towel I once found draped over me when I woke there. Then the usual panic-stricken search for phone, wallet and glasses. My wallet was in my back pocket. My glasses were on the floor over by the television as if flung there. No phone, though. Oh, good.

I had not the faintest idea what the time was. I peered out of the grimy window to try to gauge the hour by the strength of the daylight. The sky was overcast, the road empty. Difficult to tell. There wasn't a clock in the sitting room. Nor was there one in the kitchen. I opened Trev's bedroom door and crept in to look for his phone.

Trev, all head and massive, tattooed torso, was sleeping on his side, gently, like a big baby. In his bedroom's half-light, I tried to see him through the eyes of the metaphysical poet John Donne, who also admired and sought the company of what he called 'fighting and untrussed gallants'. Not that I would have lasted five minutes among those toughs in tights. I would have been mercilessly derided as 'Mr What's-the-Time?' no doubt, or as a ludicrously lightweight drinker.

I spotted Trev's phone on his bedside table next to his Lambert & Butler Golds and his disposable lighter. It was a smartphone. Not a brand I recognised. The hard casing was partially melted. I tried to wake it up. I didn't know whether to tap the screen, swipe it, or talk to it nicely. I tried all three methods and succeeded only in opening Trev's eyes. The eyelids sprang apart, instantly awake. 'All right, Bud?' he said, genially. 'What time is it?' I said.

He took the phone and activated it. 'Ten twenty-nine,' he said. He showed me the phone's home screen to prove it. Virtual raindrops were streaming down the inside. He switched on a pair of windscreen wipers that squeaked realistically and he roared with delighted laughter at the absurdity of it. My mission to pinpoint my position in time as well as space now accomplished, I walked around to the empty side of his bed, lay down on my back beside him, groaned and expired.

He reached out for a fag, poked it between his lips and put a long flame against the end. The filter was submerged entirely by Trev's encircling lips and he sucked the guts out of the fag in four or five Herculean tokes. Disposing of the collapsed remains, he promptly lit a fresh one for a more leisurely smoke.

'What time did we get back?' he said, exhaling a great nimbus plume of smoke. 'Pass,' I said. I couldn't even hazard a guess.

The pubs were quiet for a Saturday night, so we'd called a taxi and gone over to Torquay where the pubs and clubs are never quiet. Not to my knowledge. We offered the spare places in the cab to anyone in the pub who fancied an outing, and these were accepted by three total strangers: a laughing woman sitting alone at the bar, a man with a permanent, wide and apparently genuine smile, and his friend, an unsmiling unapologetically masculine woman who seemed very nice.

'How did we get home?' said Trev. 'Taxi,' I said with a momentary flash of insight. 'Don't remember it,' he said, dismissing the subject. Alighting on a much more congenial one, he said, 'The fanny in that club we went to — what was it called again? Man, it was everywhere!' 'So what happened? we've still ended up here,' I reminded him bitterly. 'Alone. Like this.' 'Your trouble is you get too pissed,' he said. 'No woman wants a bloke who gets as drunk as you do.' he said. 'And what's your excuse?' I said. 'I was doing fine!' he said indignantly. 'I was getting on like a house on fire with this one particular party. She was outside, smoking. I'd more or less pulled. And then that lesbian woman came over and stuck her nose in for some reason, she must have fancied her or something, and ruined it.' 'Well I'm blowed,' I said.

I remembered my phone. 'I've lost my phone,' I said. 'I'll ring it,' he said. 'I never thought of that,' I said.

He reached for his, scrolled through his phonebook and rang the number. I got up and tottered to the lavatory, from where I could hear that someone had answered Trev's call and was holding a cheerful conversation with him. I heard him say, 'Cheers, Bud! Cheers!' and end the call. A happy outcome by the sound of it. 'Well?' I said, returning to bed. 'Well, what?' he said. 'Well, who was it, and where were they?' I said. 'I forgot to ask,' he said. It was too early and I felt too awful to quibble. 'Coffee?' I said. 'I could try one, I suppose,' he said.

KATHLEEN BEAUCHAMP
4 October 2014

I like the New Zealand writer Katherine Mansfield, who according to Virginia Woolf smelt like a civet cat and had a hard, cheap face, and who was the only contemporary writer of whom she was remotely jealous. I like her writing and I like what I read about her short life. I'm not saying she was a great writer. I'm only saying that my imagination finds her writing voice oddly congenial. It strikes it as supremely impersonal, poker-faced and tart, with a quietly powerful undertow of sexual recklessness. But that might be just me. Funny things, writers' voices. I suppose we meet them halfway and we either embrace them or we don't. Kathleen Mansfield Beauchamp and I embraced. My favourite short story of hers, and I honestly couldn't say why, is an odd little thing never mentioned by critics called 'The Young Girl'.

In 1916, she and her husband, the utter cad and weakling John Middleton Murry, went to Provence to write. They stayed at the Hotel Beau Rivage at Bandol, near Marseilles. They had a tiff and on the third day Murray returned to London. Shortly after that she was walking alone along a stone embankment that juts out into the sea and a chap came along and chatted her up. She recorded the conversation in her notebook. This was what it was like to chat up Katherine Mansfield. 'You are alone, Madame?' 'Alone, Monsieur.' 'You are living at the hotel, Madame?' 'At the hotel, Monsieur.' 'Ah, I have noticed you walking alone several times, Madame.' 'It is possible, Monsieur.' She says the man then blushed and put his hand to his cap. 'I am very indiscreet, Madame.' 'Very indiscreet, Monsieur.'

A few weeks later, Mansfield found a cottage to rent, and Murray returned, and together they read and wrote and lived cheaply and for a few months found happiness together. The cottage was called the Villa Pauline. Last summer I visited Bandol for the afternoon and found the Villa Pauline up a side street. I leant against a hot wall and looked up at it, and screwed up my imagination and tried to see Katherine Mansfield looking out of the window at me from nearly a century before and calmly considering me. 'You are alone, Madame?'

I'm a fool like that. After I read Under the Volcano, I visited the cottage at Ripe in Sussex where Malcolm Lowry drank himself to death, and I've been twice to Virginia Woolf's surprisingly cramped house at Rodmell. I've spent the afternoon wandering around the Hemingway home at Key West in Florida. Here I noted that the prodigious number of pool laps he said he did every morning at that time were done in a pool about ten yards long. And in San Francisco the first thing I did was visit the City Lights bookstore and bar next door searching for an authentic whiff of poor Jack Kerouac. (I once met a newspaper snapper who when young was so enamoured of Kerouac that after reading On the Road he got a job as a brakeman in the San Francisco rail freight yards and stuck at it for a couple of years.)

But going back never works. Nothing lingers. When they're gone, they're gone. Even with a commemorative plaque on the wall, one is left only with a sense of vertigo at how easily all vestiges of even the recent past are obliterated and we move on. The small marble plaque on the wall of the Villa Pauline reads: 'Ici Katherine Mansfield ecrivit "Prélude". Janvier–Avril 1916.' Bandol is no longer the genteel seaside resort that it once was. And while I looked, not one of the scores of holidaymakers coming and going from the beach with towels and beach umbrellas paid the house or the plaque the slightest attention. And one wonders whether, if I had drawn to their attention that a famously innovative New Zealand writer who died young had once lived in that tiny house for three months, they would have given two hoots. And I wouldn't have blamed them if they didn't.

Last week, I succumbed to my foolishness once again and visited another of her temporary homes, this one at atmospheric Zennor in Cornwall. She and Murry came here after Bandol. In the granite cottage next door were D.H. Lawrence and Frieda. There is an amusing or perhaps rather shocking letter written by Mansfield describing how Lawrence chased Frieda around the kitchen table and tried to beat her up. I experienced the usual excitement at having found the place. And then I experienced the usual disappointment when I stood and looked and realised that Mansfield and Lawrence are so completely absent from that place that they might as well have never existed in the first place. Lawrence's cottage, I learnt from the lady at the B&B, is now occupied by the director of Tate St Ives.

HALF MOON
24 October 2014

Until a fortnight ago there was a healthy, graceful, 70ft-specimen of Eucalyptus dalrympleana — or mountain gum — in the garden. Now there isn't. Or rather, the remains of the trunk and branches are lying in sections on the ground. To knock a few quid off the tree surgeon's bill, I'd grandiosely told them not to bother reducing the trunk and major branches to fire-grate-sized logs. Leave it in rings, I said, and I'll split them up with an axe. Which they did. The next time I looked out, the men had departed and there were a couple of tons of wood lying in wheels in the sodden grass. The biggest rings, from the base of the trunk, were about two feet in diameter and a foot thick. Not a problem. A joy. I filed a razor-sharp edge on the axe-head, put the two biggest, knottiest-looking rings one on top of the other for a chopping block, and started swinging.

Why is splitting wood so supremely satisfying? Does anybody know? The first afternoon of log-splitting didn't feel like labour. The lovely tree bore me no ill-will and yielded generously to the blade. Knots were few and honest about their hidden extent. My pile of split wood grew quickly and looked as photogenic in the winter-afternoon sunlight as only a woodpile can.

My old axe and I became reacquainted. Accuracy was at first based on hope, then faith, then belief, then certainty. As confidence grew, the starting point of the axe-head moved further down my back so that full momentum could be achieved long before the axe-head reached the apogee of the arc. Each stroke of the axe meant a preliminary rough guess at the amount of force required to split the wood. My axe was a little too sharp. If I over-estimated the force required to split a log, the axe-head buried itself in the chopping block and was the devil to get out again. Otherwise it was the most pleasurable afternoon I'd spent since I'd last wielded an axe, which was couple of winters ago.

The next day, the grandson came to spend the afternoon. Right, I thought. Today would be that Holy day when man initiates boy into the mystical pleasures of manual labour. In all of his four years I don't suppose he'd seen even a hole being dug with a spade except at the beach. He was serendipitously wearing a shirt of lumberjack check. I changed into one myself. And together we walked out on to the fields of praise carrying our tools. Never give a sword to a man who can't dance, goes the old Celtic saying. Oscar can dance. (Lately he and I have been dancing deliberately and effetely to 'Love Calls' by Headstrong Feat.) He carried the axe proudly to the place of mud and white splinters, affecting nonchalance.

His first-ever job of manual labour was to gather up the wood that I'd split and throw it on the pile. To give him a rough idea of the exciting possibilities that lay before us, I selected the thickest ring and heaved it up on to the chopping block. Then I swung back and smashed it asunder and Oscar shrieked with joy and perhaps surprise at his grandad's alacrity. And then we went to work: me chopping, him chucking.

I think Oscar must have been a member of the labouring classes in his previous life. Getting his hands dirty meant nothing to him. He rolled up his sleeves to his elbows like an old navvy. He was attentive, committed, unafraid. He showed initiative and team spirit. He relished the challenge of trying the limits of his strength. He did everything but spit on his hands. He'd have been just the sort of bloke a short-staffed 19th-century mill owner would have been looking for.

If he has a fault, it is to ask too many questions. He calls me Germy. He prefaces every question with it. All too often, he would time his question for that split second when the axe-head was poised at the height of its swing and grandad was on tiptoe, concentrating every fibre as he pulled the trigger. 'Germy?' he said, on one such occasion. I pressed the emergency stop button and stood tottering on tiptoe, the axe still at the perpendicular. 'Yes,' I said as kindly as I could manage. 'Look at the moon, Germy,' he said, pointing behind me. I peered over my shoulder at it. A brilliant half-moon in a mauve evening sky. It was extraordinarily bright. So I lowered the axe and gathered my workmate up into my arms and together we observed the moon in silence for perhaps a minute, before resuming our work again.

HALLO SKY!
25 October 2014

What a beautiful day, I thought, as I nodded to the porter in the bowler hat and stepped out of the Westminster hotel into October sun and wind, with a fast-forwarding sky overhead and the crackle of leaves underfoot. Lovely London. Solid, masculine, powerful, exciting London. Beautiful London. Outside Westminster Abbey the pavements were thronged with tourists pointing their cameras and smartphones at anything and everything, from the traffic cops to the decorative spikes on the railings. Pret à Manger was packed with riot police in full battledress queueing nicely for their mid-morning caffeine fix.

I crossed over the road into Parliament Square and passed a statue of what looked like a black troll. The figure was stooped, possibly owing to the weight of its oversized head. Closer inspection revealed that it was a statue of Nelson Mandela. His outstretched hands were positioned like those of the fisherman boasting 'it was that big'. Everything about this statue — the execution, the small, democratic plinth, the aimless alignment — was comically botched. But it might have been just me. And on this lovely mid-autumn Saturday morning, I wasn't going to start making foolish judgments about art. Not when it was feeling this good to be alive and part of a London crowd, and with the added drama of a police chopper thrumming low over our heads, and the sound of hysterical drumming coming from the direction of Trafalgar Square.

Next to Nelson Mandela a copper was explaining to a sullen young Occupy activist Parliament Square's new 'no camping' laws, drawn up especially to evict the anti-war demonstrator Brian Haw, who lived in a tent on its lawn for ten years. I once spent the night with Brian Haw. He was a deep mahogany colour and rather superior. I was supposed to write about him for a newspaper. But he was supercilious towards me. The only thing he said to me all night was: 'You're drunk. I don't like drunks.' But you couldn't help respecting a man so zealous for justice that he left his wife and seven children to go and live in a tent in Parliament Square. I only hope that unlike Nelson Mandela's, Brian's statue, when he gets one, is going to have a proper plinth.

I crossed the road from beside Churchill's statue and headed up Whitehall, which was closed to traffic. Beyond the Cenotaph, and near enough to be competing with it, was a massive monument to the Women of World War II. 'Let the women of Britain come forward,' said Churchill. Seven million volunteered. And here was their monument: a forbidding 22-foot-high bronze block around which hangs a row of crudely rendered uniforms, as on a coat rack at a party. At first glance I didn't notice that the uniforms were empty and I assumed I was looking at a rendering of a gallows with multiple hangings. The thing is so brutish, Lutyens's Cenotaph looks feminine by comparison.

But what do I know about art? I don't even know what I like. And I was feeling so good, so alive, and so in love with London, that I mentally apologised to myself, God and the universe for slipping into judgmental nitwit mode again, and I headed on up the road towards the drumming and the tumults in Trafalgar Square.

The buildings of Whitehall looked splendid, almost magical in the sunshine. The north end was cordoned off to allow a demonstration by 80,000 public sector workers to pass by. I stood for half an hour and looked at the passing faces and the banners and read the placards. There it was, in the flesh: the public sector. The march was efficiently corralled by trade union stewards and not in the slightest bit confrontational. The riot police in Pret à Manger could quietly sip their coffees and maybe order a bacon, brie and pear on artisan bread to eat in. A few marchers looked enraged by what the government had done to them personally, but most were cheerful and clearly out to enjoy themselves, the nurses particularly. I was pleased to see my old trade union, the General, Municipal, Boilermakers and Allied Trade Union, march past in close formation with purposeful faces to a military-style drumbeat, exactly like marching workers on the old Soviet propaganda posters.

I stood and looked at all those sunlit public sector worker faces and felt so at peace with myself and the world that I loved these public sector marchers, every one. How beautiful London is, I thought. And how beautiful are the people in it. In a world as beautiful as this, I thought, why would anyone want to take drugs? And then I remembered that I was on drugs, and had been since yesterday, and that all this love I was feeling was probably only temporary.

ARNIE AND
THE BARONESS
20 November 2014

An hour earlier I had stepped off a plane from Dublin
and I was three-quarters deaf in one ear. I had a drink
in the bar at Boisdales Canary Wharf and a gander at
the seating plan. Fourteen to a table. I was on table 18. I
went up the stairs. Only one person was already in place:
a poised woman wearing a three-string pearl necklace.
Everyone else must have been finishing their cigars on
the terrace. My name card placed me beside her. I put
my complimentary five-pack of hand-rolled cigars on the
table, plonked myself down, and said, 'Hallo, I'm Jeremy.'
'Jean. Jean Trumpington,' she said. 'Do you smoke cigars,
Jean?' I said. 'The last time I smoked a cigar was behind a
cowshed in East Kent,' she said. 'And that was many, many
years ago.' Further conversation revealed the startling fact
that she was Baroness Trumpington, agriculture minister
in Lady Thatcher's government. 'Have you ever been to
the House of Lords,' she said. 'Nope,' I said. 'Then you
must come to tea,' she said.

The vast room now filled with people wearing evening
dress searching for their tables and places. A pleasant chap
seated himself on my left and introduced himself as Tom.
He enjoyed reading The Spectator, he said, particularly
the Low life column. I asked him what he did. He was a
restaurant critic, he said. And then Arnold Schwarzenegger
appeared like a tanned, solid-looking genie, right in front
of us. I could have reached out and caressed him. This

was the Spectator Cigar Smoker of the Year 2014 awards and the Terminator was a nominee, apparently. He smiled unflinchingly into the repeated volleys of the jostling photographers' flashguns.

'Is that Arnie?' said the Baroness. I said that it was. As we were both a little deaf we had to put our heads together to make ourselves heard above the rising hubbub. 'Now listen,' she said. 'I want you to introduce me to him. I must have my photograph taken with him to show my neighbours. The people upstairs are terribly excited about me being in same room as Arnold Schwarzenegger and I need proof or they won't believe me. Will you do that?' I agreed, but was made redundant from my job almost immediately because Arnie gallantly came over to introduce himself to her. The phalanx of snappers followed him over and they took about 500 photographs of Arnie bending from the waist to introduce himself to the seated Baroness. 'Get out of the way!' chorused the snappers to me.

Arnie returned to his table and dinner was served. The pleasant bloke on my right was reminiscing with a chap opposite about the comedian Peter Cook. I poked the Baroness with an elbow and said, 'This chap on the other side of me: do you know him?' 'Tom? Yes, as a matter of fact I do,' she said. 'His mother is married to the Prince of Wales.' 'I see,' I said, sticking another forkful of white crabmeat into my gob.

A chap with a neat beard seated opposite the Baroness and me, three seats to the right, was also a cynosure. The snappers kept coming and massacring him with their flashguns, and various individuals sidled up to his chair and shyly asked for his blessing. 'Who's that?' said the

Baroness. 'Hang on,' I said. I turned to Tom. 'Tom,' I said. 'Who's that over there? Him with the beard arrangement.' 'It's Kelsey Grammer,' he said. 'Remember Frasier, the hit US sitcom? Him. Please excuse me,' he said, rising from his chair. 'I'm the compère and it's time for me to get up on stage.' So he went off, and Frasier, perhaps needing to spread himself out bit, spotted Tom's empty chair and came and occupied it. 'Are you Frasier?' I said. Smiling affably, he smartly extended a ramrod forearm with a huge and hygienically clean hand on the end. I said, 'Are you going out tonight, Frasier? Because if you are, don't go without me.' 'Well,' he said. 'I think that a few of us maybe have a sort of a plan to go on somewhere.' 'Count me in,' I said. 'Don't,' I said sternly, 'leave without me.' He promised faithfully. I turned to the Baroness and reported the encounter to her. She listened carefully, fascinated. 'Why don't you come with us, Jean?' I said. 'I'm going home to bed,' she said firmly. 'I'm getting up and going to Waitrose in the morning.'

And then I heard my name mentioned from the podium. 'What did he say, Jean?' I said. 'You are presenting the first award,' she said. 'Jolly good luck.'

So I went up on the stage and did that. And the evening went on like that, with one pleasant surprise after another, and it was one of the most fantastic evenings ever.

HIMANDHOO
29 November 2014

We clambered aboard a dhoni, the sturdy wooden boat that the Maldivians use for getting about the islands, and motored across from our high-end 'all-inclusive' resort to a 'traditional' island village for a guided tour. Maldivians are devout Muslims and it was suggested to us that we dress modestly and behave respectfully when there. Our guide was Mohamed, a self-confident 22-year-old fisherman. 'Ask me anything. I know everything,' he said.

His village was called Himandhoo. According to Mohamed, it means 'fishing village'. He led us first to the village school. The writing on the classroom walls was Thaana, a peculiar script resembling a cross between shorthand and Arabic. Words are read from right to left; numbers from left to right. 'How many letters are there in your alphabet?' someone asked him. Our omniscient guide had to think long and hard about that one. 'I don't know,' he said. 'I think between 28 and 36. I was not very good at my language at school. I only got a C. I was better at English and got a B.' He then related with great pride how he often used to climb out of the window when the teacher had his back turned and go fishing. 'Were you ever punished?' I said. 'Beaten with a cane?' He was astonished by the idea. 'No, no,' he said. 'Certainly not. We don't do that here. Once the teacher made me stand out in the sun at noon for an hour. Another time he made me stand with my arms stretched out and hung a brick on each arm and I had to stand there like that. But no, no beating. We don't do that.'

The sandy streets were narrow and the women we saw walked quickly, their burkas billowing out behind them. Soon we came to a small building painted a vivid turquoise. Above the door was written in English: Magistrates Court. 'Tell me,' he said. 'For what purpose do we use this building?' 'For trying criminals?' ventured someone. 'For marriage,' he said. 'Only for marriage. I myself hope to come here one day. We marry here usually at around 24 or 25.' 'What about sex before marriage?' I said. 'Is it allowed?' 'No,' he said. 'If you have sex before marriage and you are caught, a man will come to your house and hit you 80 times on your behind with a bat. If you are caught a second time, both you and the woman will be buried up to your necks and everyone will throw stones at your heads until you are both dead.' 'And so when was the last time this happened in the village?' I said. 'Never!' he laughed. 'Why would anyone want to break the law when you are punished like that.'

On a lighter note, he pointed to an ancient banyan tree and asked us to guess how old it was. Someone guessed a thousand years. 'Three hundred,' he said. 'When I was a child, I used to hide from the teachers up there. Look up and you can see where the branches make a platform.' We craned upwards and saw a knot of branches about 30 feet up. 'Once I fell out, but I was OK,' he said.

We walked on until we came to a very overgrown plot with a few headstones visible. 'This is our cemetery,' he said. 'Women are not allowed in here, not even to mourn. If they want to mourn and cry, they can do that at home or at the mosque.' 'They aren't allowed to go in here,' said a female member of our group with a touch of steely irony, 'but are they allowed to be buried in here?' 'Yes,' said Mohamed magnanimously. 'They are allowed in when they are dead. When we are dead, everybody can come in, even women.'

The houses were mostly windowless. Some were without doors or even a front wall and you could see the women inside sitting on the floor weaving coconut mats. In Mohamed's house a young woman with a life of unremitting toil written all over her face was sitting on the floor weaving coconut mats. She looked up at us with the same expression of wariness, suspicion and incomprehension that you might see on a mistreated dog. Mohamed neither greeted nor acknowledged her. 'Your mother?' I said. 'A neighbour,' he said.

Back aboard the dhoni for the return journey, I asked Mohamed what the people of his village did for recreation seeing that alcohol is banned. Did they smoke weed, for example? 'Only heroin,' he said. Until now, Mohamed had answered our questions with a sort of deadpan levity. Here, unexpectedly, he was speaking from the heart. 'Is a very big problem here in the Maldives," he said. 'And I hate it. I really hate it."

MEET THE HACKS
6 December 2014

The thing I enjoy most about travel-writing gigs is meeting other hacks. Hacks are almost invariably fun, funny, gossipy, irreverent, and they like a drink. They are well read and intelligent, but like to conceal it. They know and understand the lineaments of power as well as politicians, only they think it's funny. On multi-hack travel gigs you can tell whether there is a drain or a nutcase in the squad during the introductions in the Heathrow departures lounge. In this case we could safely sound the 'all-clear'. The line-up consisted of a man from the *Daily Mail*, a woman from the *Daily Telegraph*, a woman from the *Sunday Times* and myself.

In his 50 years, the *Mail* man has so far visited 134 countries, mostly as an independent traveller. Sir Richard Burton is one of his heroes, and to hear the *Mail* man's tales, he is without doubt as great a traveller as the Satanic-faced Victorian, and he has similar passions, especially for the Islamic countries, though he lacks Burton's amazing facility for languages. You can say what you like about the *Daily Mail*, but if that man is a typical representative of its travel section, it must be a far more enlightened newspaper than many give it credit for. Name a country — any country, hot or cold — and he had been there. He was unpretentious, unassuming and without prejudices.

In her way, the woman from the *Telegraph* was equally spectacular. The *Daily Telegraph* is (in my limited experience) a remarkable mixture of toffs and Essex girls and boys, and this woman was a working-class Essex girl. She had been absolutely everywhere, but without losing a shred of her class identity or cool. One morning I was lounging about near the diving-school headquarters. That morning's boat party was already assembled and she had yet to appear. I heard a German woman say, 'I consider myself to be a normal, nice person. But lateness of this order is something I cannot tolerate.' Five minutes later up came Natalie from Colchester with her laid-back, stoner gait, smoking a fag. 'Alright?' she said, cheerfully flicking away the stub and totally oblivious to the hostile glares. The *Sunday Times* travel reporter, too, was a chrome-plated hack in possession of a limitless fund of newspaper and celebrity gossip, which she imparted with an inventive turn of phrase, comic timing and a gift for mimicry. She was also kind-hearted and a bit of a lefty.

And finally there was your Low life correspondent, who established himself early on as a kind of unsurpassable benchmark of naivety and unsophistication. Example one: when selected by the waiter to sample the wine on behalf of the company, I got into a tizzy, picked up my glass of water instead, sampled it carefully and expertly, and sincerely pronounced it 'superb'. Example two: my daily reports of gains made using my NHS-prescribed erectile dysfunction vacuum pump, which I'd brought on holiday with me as my partner.

We all got on like a high-end resort bungalow on fire. Every breakfast, lunch and dinner was a prolonged affair, until we seemed to spend almost the entire day barefoot at the beachside meal table drinking wine and entertaining each other with stories. In the evenings, we were usually joined by a smiling resort representative. Among others, there was Nadine from Mauritius, Connie from Taiwan, and Takiko from Japan. These were politely attended to at first, then rather overwhelmed, I am sorry to say, by the vinous ebb and flow. Takiko, for example, bowed and giggled and nodded throughout the meal with more goodwill than comprehension, then broke the habit of a lifetime by drinking an entire second glass of wine, after which her bowing and giggling redoubled, while mentally she appeared to retreat into a very sweet and private ecstasy.

Halfway through the week, sadly, Natalie flew back home and was replaced by another travel journalist. And it was as if we'd sold our best striker and replaced her with my nan. She was not only a purveyor of that kind of meaningless purple travel prose that is a foretaste of death, but she actually believed it. If I sound snobby, it is because I am. From then on, that end of the table was for martyrs only. The man from the *Mail* — perhaps the most sociable man the world has ever known — threw himself on the grenade whenever he could by taking the vacant place at the table opposite her. But even he was cowed into miserable silence by a barrage of almost inconceivable blandness. But who am I to judge? And at least it got us off our backsides to wander among the whispering palms or swim in the azure sea.

BLOODY CHAUCER
3 January 2015

A fruity voice on the train's announcement system said, 'Ladies and gentlemen, make sure you have all your belongings, family members and what have you with you when alighting from the train. We are now arriving in the naughty little station of Newton Abbot.' This carriage was empty. The Teign estuary sparkled in the Sunday morning sunshine. The line from Totnes in Devon to Paddington is a lovely journey at any time of the year across the farms and pastures green of Devon, Somerset, Wiltshire and Berkshire. Always I have good intentions to read, but usually I rest my chin on the heel of my palm and look out of the window for the entire journey, giving leisurely thought to non-urgent matters, or fantasising, or simply letting the passing English countryside speak to its most fervent admirer. Having said my sad goodbyes in the station car park, while my grandson spray-spewed all over the back seat of my son's car, I was in that meditative frame of mind now.

As we neared Exeter, a perfect rainbow arising from the medieval cathedral's lead roof parenthesised the city. So that's another year gone by, I thought, and I'm still alive and kicking. I haven't written about my cancer here — thank the Lord! I hear you say. I've written about my cancer business instead in a weekly column for a Sunday newspaper magazine. Me and my cancer, week in week out. Strewth. But a few weeks ago the editor wrote me a

230

brief email saying that they have had all they can stand of it. The magazine was having a 'refresh' in the new year and my column 'hadn't made' the back page, she said. (She introduced herself as my editor for the past few months, though I'd never even heard of her.)

I didn't blame the poor woman. Even if bloody Chaucer wrote a cancer column every week for the Sunday papers, it would quickly pall, and I was genuinely amazed that I'd lasted a whole year. But the money: oh, the money! Throughout 2014 I was getting £600 a week on top of my *Spectator* pay, which might not sound a lot to you *Spectator* readers, but that 26 grand changed my life. I bought three cars, wore new clothes, and was spoken to more nicely by the kind of people who narrow their eyes and make on-the-spot calculations about their interlocutor's wealth. I bought stuff on Amazon while lying in bed in the morning, and, moron that I am, I believed that I had gone up in the world and was now a person of consequence.

The camp voice on the loudspeaker piped up again to announce that we were now arriving in 'exciting' Exeter. Seconds later, the voice's owner appeared at my side asking to see my ticket. Silver earrings (both ears); enamel rainbows for cufflinks. 'Any idea which way to the buffet?' I said. 'There's a trolley service only, I'm afraid, sir,' he said. 'You can't miss her when she comes clattering through the doors. She's a little peach!' Then he was gone, and I looked out of the window again and pondered some more on my miraculous year; a year of life when I expected to be pushing up the daisies; a year of stubborn good health; a year of, well, euphoria.

Of love, too. The other day I read A.N. Wilson's terrific biography of Hitler in a sitting. While considering Hitler's love life, A.N. Wilson offers the following aside concerning the nature of love. 'The British poet Stevie Smith, who led a maidenly existence, unmarried, in a dull suburb of north London, once angrily reacted to a person who told her she did not have any experience of love. "I do," she replied. "I love my aunt." Love,' A.N. Wilson levelly reminds us, 'takes many forms.'

This past year, I have been consumed by a love affair with my grandson. He's had a difficult year adjusting to Mummy not liking Daddy any more, then finding someone she does like, and last weekend marrying him instead. So I talk to my grandson about his life, and about life in general, and I run a few popular philosophies of life past him to see what he thinks. He's five. Driving home in the dark the other day, I was giving him a sententious little lecture about how lucky we are to have been born in 21st-century England, where there's enough to eat. 'I'm not bothered about having enough to eat,' he said. 'I'm just glad I was born with you.'

With a tremendous clatter, the buffet trolley appeared in the carriage, recklessly driven by the peach. I flagged him down. I was very glad to see him, I told him, because I was Hank Marvin. And for the first time in a year, my choice of fare was dictated to a certain extent by the cost.

CHOOSING DICK
7 January 2015

The hotel and its bright tan prayer rug of a beach were one. In the early morning the distant image of Cannes, the pink and cream of old fortifications, the purple Alp that bounded Italy, were cast across the water and lay quivering in the ripples and rings sent up by sea-plants through the clear shallows.

Recognise it? F. Scott Fitzgerald's *Tender is the Night*. First page. Hollywood starlet Rosemary Hoyt and her mentoring mother take ground-floor rooms at a quiet beachside Antibes hotel. Rosemary wanders out and on to the aforementioned beach, takes off her bathing robe, wades into a 'blue as laundry water' sea, then 'laid her face on the water and swam a choppy four-beat crawl out to the raft'. Returning ashore, she finds a space on the beach beside a party of rich and languid Americans, spreads out her peignoir on the sand, and lies down to sunbathe.

'Lying so, she first heard their voices and felt their feet skirt her body and their shapes pass between the sun and herself. The breath of an inquisitive dog blew warm and nervous on her neck.'

I love that inquisitive dog. Who hasn't sunbathed on a beach with eyes closed and felt that warm, nervous snuffling? The unfolding story is Rosemary's growing infatuation with Dick, the leader of the languid ones. And I have loved Scott Fitzgerald's pine-fringed prayer rug of a beach ever since I read his patchy novel for the first time in my twenties. That fictional Riviera beach stands out more vividly in my imagination than most of the real ones I've sat on. So, as you might imagine, I was rather excited, while staying last week in Antibes, and idly browsing the web for tourist information, to read that a west-facing Antibes beach called la Garoupe is the selfsame beach described by Fitzgerald at the beginning of Tender is the Night. The link was credible, too. Not every local website that stood to gain commercially by such a glamorous connection seemed aware of it. Apparently, Scott and Zelda rented a succession of villas between St Raphael and Antibes and used to frequent la Garoupe.

I am a literary pilgrim of the most open-mouthed sort. It must be a type of cretinism to enjoy fiction and then physically to visit the settings and to want so badly that the fictions be somehow present and tangible. Perhaps it is a vice akin to masturbation. And here at Antibes, I now discovered, a mile from the hotel, just beyond the pines on the headland, is my everyone gone out, have a soak in the bath first, put some music on wank of the decade.

I jumped in the car. At the end of the coast road was a narrow, sandy car park bordered by a high chain-link fence through which I could see a tatty restaurant (shut for the winter) overlooking a tiny, narrow crescent beach — la Plage de la Garoupe. The beach was prettily encircled by opposing headlands. Five miles away across smooth water I could see the hideous concrete sprawl of Cannes and Nice, and behind these the French Alps, their snowy peaks against a cloudless Mediterranean winter sky. If I shut one eye and half-closed the other, and ignored the car park and dilapidated restaurant, and the EasyJet airliner with its undercarriage down coming in to land at Nice airport; and if I made allowance for the unsightly heaps of sand at the back of the beach, bulldozed there to preserve it all from being scattered by the winter storms; and if I forgave the beach's disappointing narrowness and tried to convince myself that this was a hot July morning, the dew on the pines evaporating rapidly, then yes! actually, yes!, it was possible to see Dick Diver in his jockey cap raking pebbles from the sand with a burlesque show of seriousness and application, and laconic Abe North, and Tommy Barban reading aloud and cynically from the local newspaper, and Nicole's pearls against her tan, and the gaudy changing-tent, and the inflatable rubber horse, and the beach umbrellas, and Rosemary Hoyt lying on her back choosing Dick with her eyes.

The next morning, mining the web again for local information, I was surprised to read that Graham Greene, no less, lived in Antibes for 24 years, from 1966 until 1990. I dashed out right away and eventually found La Résidence des Fleurs in Avenue Pasteur and asked a passer-by to snap me leaning against the small, rather curt commemorative plaque. And even though it has probably changed hands 15 times since then, I went for lunch, as Grim Grin did almost every day, at the Cafe Felix, beside the south port gate.

I tell you, it's at best a vice and at worst a sickness, this thing I have. And so boring for others.

TAXI!
24 January 2015

The taxi-driver wound his window one third of the way down and put a priestlike, confessional ear to the freezing night air. I spoke the name of my village. Twelve miles. Twenty minutes. Forty quid normally, including tip. A decent fare, considering that the vast majority waiting at this railway-station cab rank require only the short ride into town. And yet an agonised grimace contorted his miserable, flabby, unshaved face. After an omnipotent pause, however, it nodded gloomy assent and I walked around the bonnet of the 12-year-old Mondeo and climbed into the passenger seat.

'Busy?' I said when we were in motion, to start the conversational ball rolling. He slumped forward on his steering wheel in despair and looked at me as if I was mad asking that on a January midweek night as cold and as wet as this one. 'Good Christmas?' I said, trying to force a cheerful word out of the guy. Not that either. He hadn't had a good Christmas, he said, because last summer his wife had walked out on him after 20 years and gone to live with the boyfriend she'd had when they were at school together. He had come home from a busy day's taxiing and found a note on the kitchen table saying, 'I don't love you any more. I'm going to live with Ian.'

He was still numb, he said. Indeed he looked it. Then I got the full jeremiad. For 20 years he'd worked his fingers to the bone. She and the two kids had wanted for fuck all.

And then, right out of the blue, she'd done that, he said. 'You ask me if I had a good fucking Christmas?' he said. 'Waking up on fucking Christmas Day on your own for the first time in your fucking life? No, not fucking really, is the answer to that one, my friend.'

The novelist Anthony Powell once said that the essential ingredient of any bestseller is self-pity. If true, this guy ought to turn his hand to fiction because he'd very quickly have a runaway success on his hands. Steering our conversation always towards the light, I asked him whether New Year's Eve had been busy and profitable for him. The memory of New Year's Eve depressed him almost as much as his wife leaving. He had been busy, yes. He didn't stop from six o'fucking clock in the evening until ten o'clock on New Year's Day. Then he went home and lay down on the bed too tired to take off his clothes or eat and he slept for 12 hours.

'One drunk after another, I suppose,' I said. 'Was anybody sick in the back?' No, nobody was sick in the back, he said, but he did have one interesting story. He'd picked up this couple, and the woman was climbing all over the bloke in the back for the entire journey. Couldn't keep her hands off him. Two days later he picked up the same woman, only now with a different man — her husband, he thinks, because they weren't touching at all. Also, for the entire journey she was meeting his eyes in the rear-view mirror pleading with them for him not to say anything. And two days after that he picked her up with the first bloke and she's eating him alive again from the word go.

'What did she look like?' I said. 'Would you fuck her?' He considered the question in all its various aspects and implications very thoroughly before coming to a decision. 'No,' he said. 'Why not?' I said. He pondered some more. Finally he said, 'Because she was cheap, if you know what I mean.' 'Cheap?' I said, genuinely surprised. 'How do you mean — cheap?' 'Well, she was foul-mouthed for one thing,' he said. 'It was all "fucking this" and "fucking that". Every time she opened her mouth. Horrible to hear a woman swearing like that.' 'Fucking hell,' I said.

For 12 miles I tried to get this decent man to say something positive; to confess a delight in his life; but he was indefatigably miserable. In a last-ditch attempt to cheer him up, I said, 'I've got cancer.' He looked at me with redoubled seriousness. 'Fuck off,' he said. 'But I have,' I said. 'Nymphs and shepherds dance no more.' 'Nymphos and what?' he said. 'Shepherds,' I said. There was a silence between us while he tried to unravel my meaning. But of this unfair and incomprehensible world he was understanding less and less these days. 'Oh, shepherds,' he said. Then, darting his melancholy eyes between the radio and the road ahead, he turned the music up a couple of notches.

WINE CLUB
7 February 2015

This month's wine club lecture was on red burgundy. The members were settling themselves at two large tables when I arrived, about ten to each one. I took an empty seat at the table farthest from the door and looked diffidently around, hoping to meet a welcoming eye. Not one. Presumably members were tired of sharing the mysteries of their deity with people who came only once, and they had evolved a wait-and-see policy.

Everyone had brought their own wine glass. There were glasses of every size and shape. Most had a notebook and biro also at the ready. The woman sitting directly opposite me now spoke to me accusingly. 'Where's your glass?' she said. I shrugged at her. 'Didn't you read the flier? It clearly says to bring a glass and knife. You'll have to go and ask that man over there if he can find you one.' So I humbly went and asked the chap she had pointed out if I could borrow a wine glass. Without a word he went and got me one and handed it over in a deliberately non-judgmental manner.

I retook my seat and placed my borrowed wine glass on the table. For a wine glass it was very small. Beside the woman on my right's gigantic goblet, it looked ridiculous. The lecturer, standing beside a counter with bottles lined up, then commenced to talk about our first red burgundy of the evening, and those with notebook and pen began scribbling. About the first wine I can remember only that it was a 2012 village burgundy. The lecturer was extremely knowledgable and spoke eloquently. He seemed to know the 2012 harvest grape by individual grape. Once, he became emotional and his speech faltered. After stretching the majority of attention spans to well beyond breaking point, he finally came around the tables and tipped a couple of blood-red mouthfuls into each glass. At last the wine club could begin their worship with nose and palate.

Self-consciously, I buried my bugle into my wine glass and with bulging eyeballs sniffed fanatically at the liquid in the bottom. I lowered the glass and pondered. I sniffed again at the wine, more delicately this time. Then I slung the contents of my glass down my open throat, tilting my head back until the glass was upside-down, afterwards straining my head back as far as it would go to let fall that last recalcitrant drop. Yes, it was red wine, and without a doubt.

Centrally placed on each table was an aluminium spittoon. My neighbour with the big goblet took this spittoon in both hands and carefully dribbled rather than spat her wine into it, the only one on our table to do so. We were swallowers on our table rather than spitters. With nothing to compare it with, members were loath to commit themselves to a forthright pronouncement on this first village red. They were keeping their powder dry. A watery-eyed old gentleman, however, ventured the opinion that it was his favourite wine of the evening so far.

By about the sixth or seventh sampling, the members were loosening up noticeably. The spirit was moving among them. Opinions were being bandied and there were amiable controversies. The woman opposite, so impersonal and legalistic to begin with, was now euphoric and couldn't care less about anything. 'What year did he say that last one was?' she said, biro hovering. 'Eighteen-nineteen,' I said. She had started to write it down then realised it was a joke and fell about, delighted by her gullibility. The watery-eyed old gentleman was now saying after each and every wine that it was his favourite wine of the evening so far. And everybody confessed that they felt exactly the same way, even though it was silly.

The woman with the big goblet then put me on the spot by asking my opinion of the wine we had most recently tasted. I said that they all tasted more or less the same to me. She corrected me, saying that it was on the nose rather than on the palate that wine distinguishes itself. I said I'd had two lines of coke before I came out, so was probably at a disadvantage. For a split second she wasn't sure if this was a joke or not, decided that it was, that it had to be, and laughed. Now such a hubbub of conversation and laughter arose during each sampling that the lecturer had to rap repeatedly on an empty bottle with a knife to restore order.

We sampled ten red burgundies altogether. I was quite pissed by the end. And in the end, too, I had a mysterious sense that I had unknowingly passed a test, had been recognised as a co-religionist (though a rude one), and been welcomed into the fellowship.

HOTEL REVIEW: TRIPADVISOR
21 February 2015

This hotel is brand new. One half is a university students' hostel, the other an apartment hotel. Car parking is ample and free of charge. The students we saw coming and going from the lobby were easily our social superiors. The check-in guy was clean and polite, and without being asked supplied us with a free map of the town centre and marked our position with a biro cross. Although a functionary, this man was also our social superior. 'Are you here for business or pleasure, madam?' he asked my companion. She and I hadn't actually met until about half an hour earlier and our intention was to quickly get to know one another as soon as the door of the room had closed behind us, maybe go out for something to eat later, then come back and carry on getting to know each other. 'Business, babe,' she laughed.

The whole check-in experience was fast, easy and smooth. Though situated right next to the railway station, the apartments were more than adequately insulated against noise from outside and from each other. Ours was spotlessly clean and the kitchen area well equipped. Sachets of tea and coffee were provided, also shortbread biscuits, over which we had our first small disagreement. I picked up the remote and flicked on the adequate-sized telly. The BBC News Channel with subtitles for the hard of hearing came up. I kept it on without the sound, and watched a clip of some pro-Russian or very Russian rebels silently shelling Ukrainian positions. Then we started to get to know one another.

We began in the unambiguous way in which they generally begin in pornography films. In musical terms, if I may, her embouchure and handling were virtuoso, the arrangement a rhapsody accelerando with finale. Her repertoire included tremolo and glissando. The mood varied from dolente to furioso to delirio.

During one of the slow movements, I looked up and saw that the news had been paused for a weather forecast. Interested, I studied the symbols on the weatherman's map and carefully watched his pointing arm and read the subtitles for the deaf and hard of hearing underneath. The subtitles were computer-generated using speech-recognition software. If in doubt about a word used by the cheerful weatherman, the computer plumped for the word that it had used the most often before in its career. In our part of the country, then, after a wet start tomorrow, we were going to enjoy 'Sunni intervals'. So that was good. Northern Ireland, too, could look forward to 'the cloud partially clearing from the west and Sunni spells' from mid-afternoon onwards.

After a while we dispensed with polite formalities and got on with it. At one point I thought she said, 'That hurts,' and I stopped immediately. But I'm getting a little deaf in my old age and what she'd actually said was, 'Hurt me'. Later she said, 'I'm hungry. Are you?' I agreed that I was, very, and we got ready to go out and look for somewhere to eat. She went first into the spacious and well-appointed bath and shower room. Everything in it was brand new. The heated towel rail was scalding hot, which was great. The bathroom was off the kitchen, separated from it by a sliding door.

Presently there came piercing shrieks from the bathroom. I rushed through and flung back the sliding door. The room was fogged with steam and the floor awash with hot water. Walls, mirror, lavatory and ceiling were streaming. She had reached into the glass-sided shower cubicle and pulled the chrome tap lever, apparently, and the hot water had come out of the shower head with the force of a water cannon. The shower head had leapt out of its retaining bracket and it and its flexible pipe were thrashing about like a mortally wounded snake. Her attempts to reach in and grab the dancing shower head had ended in soaking failure. Now mine did too. The water issued from the nozzle with such violent force that I was beaten back by it twice. Only by feinting and coming at it from underneath could I get the lever tap shut, by which time the kitchen floor and part of the bedroom floor, as well as the bathroom floor, were flooded.

The suddenness of the drama and the appalling consequences were surreal. As we stood in the steaming, soaking bathroom looking at each other, she looked strangely exalted. Then, quite unexpectedly, she took a swing and punched me in the mouth out of sheer exuberance, and I went out to eat with a fat lip.

I am not normally the type of person to post on TripAdvisor. But please be warned, the showers in this otherwise perfectly acceptable hotel are verging on the dangerous.